GOLF'S
8 SECOND SECRET
WHAT SEPARATES GOLF'S GREATEST CHAMPIONS

MIKE BENDER
AND MICHAEL MERCIER

Lawless Publishing, LLC.
Florida

www.Golfs8SecondSecret.com

Lawless Publishing, LLC
530 Ocean Drive #501
Juno Beach, FL 33408

Copyright © 2016 by Mike Bender and Michael Mercier

All rights reserved. In accordance with the U.S. Copyright Act of 1976, the scanning, uploading, and electronic sharing of any part of this book without permission of the publisher constitute unlawful piracy and theft of the authors' intellectual property. If you would like to use material from the book (other than for review purposes), prior written permission must be obtained by contacting the publisher at info@lawlesspublishing.com.
Thank you for your support of the authors' rights.

ISBN 978-0-9967-1162-3

First edition: April 2016
Designer: Connor Smith
Set in Minion Pro

I would like to thank my wife Mary Anne and my daughter Hannah for allowing me the time to finish this book. Without their patience and understanding most of my projects would never be completed.

CONTENTS

Introduction 1

Chapter 1 – Mickelson & Westwood 6
Summary points 14

Chapter 2 – A New Way to Think About the Swing 15
Phase One: Information Gathering 15
Phase Two: The Pre-Swing 17
Phase Three: The Swing 23
List of Greatest Champions 26
Decline of Feel in Today's Modern Golf 28
Pressure 33
Summary Points 35

Chapter 3 – Information Gathering (Phase One) 37
Trouble on the 12th 38
The Information Gathering Phase 40
Establishing Your Club Distances 42
Pre-Round Analysis- Day Of 43
In Round Analysis 46
Flight Path & Visualization 55
Example Scenario 56
Summary Points 61

Chapter 4 – The Pre-Swing (Phase Two) 63
Time Limitation 65
Movement 66
Shot Visualization 67

Feel 70
Mechanical Swing Thoughts 71
Trigger 72
Practice Swing 72
Putting the Pieces Together 74
Maintaining a Routine 75
Summary Points 76

Chapter 5 – The Swing Phase (Phase Three) 77
It's a Matter of Time! 78
Nicklaus 80
Movement, Movement, Movement 81
Visualization & Physical Feel Strengthens Focus & Concentration 82
How to Perform the Swing Phase 84
The Waggle 86
Weight Shifting 87
Rotating Your Head 87
The Union 88
Summary Points 89

Chapter 6 – Concluding Remarks 91
What Led to Golf's 8 Second Secret 93
Essential Qualities 93
The Zone 98
Practice 100
The Full Picture 107
Summary Points 108
Inverted Triangle 109
Shot Process Chart 110

Introduction

SINCE THE INCEPTION of major championship golf, only 19 male players have won 5 or more major championships, starting with John Henry Taylor's win in the 1894 Open Championship, and most recently with Phil Mickelson's victory at the 2013 Open Championship. Think about that for a moment… We define these players as golf's greatest champions. It's quite obvious that the greatest golfers on this list (and we'll show you who they are later on) consistently performed at a higher level than their peers time and time again, but ironically, many of them did not exhibit textbook swing mechanics. So what is it that allowed these golfers, to name several: Bobby Jones, Arnold Palmer, Lee Trevino, Tom Watson, Tiger Woods, Phil Mickelson, and their female counterparts such as: Mickey Wright, Annika Sorenstam, & Julie Inkster, to achieve such a level of rare and great accomplishments? Golf's 8 Second Secret is a shot process primarily developed from the observable characteristics and written commentary of golf's greatest champions. This book teaches a shot process that we believe is similar to the shot process inherently used by the greats, which allowed them to achieve the number of wins they did. Clearly all of these great champions maximized their talents. However, the inspiring realization for any golfer who desires to improve is that the success of these golf greats was not solely predicated on actual swing mechanics.

Bobby Jones once said, "Competitive golf is played mainly on a five-and-a-half-inch course, the space between your ears." A common belief in golf is that the better your swing mechanics are, the more important the mental side of golf becomes. Most people that have been exposed to the game to any degree would concede to this. But what is it that makes golf so much more mental than any other sport? If you observe most sports, generally speaking, the best players simply react to what happens around them; furthermore, the more instinctively they react, the better they perform, especially under pressure. In golf, this is not the case… or is it?

As we know, for the most part, golfers have no time restrictions with their "traditional pre-shot routines," and can swing whenever they feel ready. Virtually no sense of urgency exists, thus limiting instinctive athletic prowess, and why should any urgency exist? Golfers do not have opposing players actively trying to steal the ball, knock them down, or block the target. In addition, the ball is not moving. Mariano Rivera is not throwing you a 90+ mph fastball. As a result, golfers can take their time. They swing when they think they are mentally prepared and physically ready. On the surface, this appears to be an advantage for players. The concession of an otherwise difficult game is that golfers have all the time in the world to strike the ball and the ball isn't moving. In Golf's 8 Second Secret, we will show that this is one of the confounding obstacles that make the game more difficult than it needs to be, and why many players do not achieve their potential. It is likely that the majority of players never recognize this. As a result, they are constantly playing in a very conscious state, thus restricting their athletic ability and their instincts.

We believe that most of the greatest golfers, if not all of them, recognized this truth about the game. For the greats, it appears that they naturally developed a shot process to combat this issue. Amazingly, two key components in nearly all their shot process' are consistently performed, which are time limitations and athletic movements. Unrestricted time and lack of sufficient movement in the shot process allows the vast majority of players to stand over each shot with the hope of using conscious mechanical swing thoughts to try to produce quality swings.

When you play a round of golf, depending on your handicap, you are only going to execute between 35 and 55 full swings. The rest of your shots will be pitches, chips and putts whose actions and movements are not complete enough to impact your full swing. In addition, aside from the shot variables, i.e. wind direction and speed, lie of the ball, etc., the majority of your swings will be "stock" swings (a normal and complete swing), and as such, for the most part, your swings should be similar to one another. Therefore, there's no sense in debilitating yourself by standing over your shots and solely centering your thinking on the numerous mechanical swing thoughts before striking your ball. If you do, you will be thinking consciously when your objective should be to execute a primarily subconscious swing which will be freer and more instinctive/reactive.

As someone who has been around the game of golf for more than 47 years, both as a player and as an instructor, I still find it amazing how different the results can be from the driving range, to the first tee, and beyond. There's something about how we perform swings when there are no consequences on the line versus when we only have one crack at hitting the correct shot with a good swing. This is not only evidenced by the differences players exhibit from the driving range to the first tee, but particularly when playing well up until the last few holes of an important round or until a pressure filled final round of a tournament. These are telltale signs of a weak shot process. Every caliber of player experiences this, from PGA Tour Winners on down. Fear and pressure can take their toll and dramatically alter both the mental and physical aspects of a weak or flawed traditional shot process.

Golf's 8 Second Secret shot process as outlined in this book consists of three phases and four key elements. The phases are: the **Information Gathering phase**, the **Pre-Swing phase** & the **Swing phase**. The key elements within two of the phases are: **time limitation**, **movement**, **shot visualization** and **feel**. The shot process starts from the moment a player begins to analyze any shot to be played (excluding putting) and ends when the follow through is completed. While we're not positive that all of the greats demonstrated all of the phases and elements, we do believe that all of them, with one exception, incorporated both similar time limitation and athletic movements in the Swing phase.

It's well known that the traditional shot process is made up of both a golfer's mental thoughts and swing mechanics, but what is far less discussed and taught is how they can work together and act as a catalyst to produce consistent high quality golf shots (even when under pressure). It's apparent that when the two do not work in conjunction, your golf shots will suffer (especially when under pressure). Over the past 25 years, I have come to realize that helping a golfer improve his swing mechanics is only as good as his ability to transfer those skills onto the golf course. If a student takes lessons to improve

Introduction

their swing, but never learns how to swing freely while under pressure, they will not play up to their potential.

Over the course of this book, we will lay out the details of the shot process we have developed and how the greats worked within this process. This process will yield many benefits. Once the three phases and the elements within each phase are learned to the point that they become second nature even under pressure, it will allow you to significantly elevate your game. You will swing more subconsciously/instinctively, which will initially give you the ability to acquire more confidence and freer swings, thus yielding higher quality shots and lower scores. Secondly, once you experience a few good rounds of increased confidence, freer swings, etc., you will have the best chance to get closer to or into the "zone." When you're in "the zone", you will achieve your potential, and at times, may even exceed your potential. The great players assuredly must have done this on a very consistent basis (i.e. played in "the zone") in order to win multiple majors.

I am very excited about the shot process presented here and how much it will help golfers bridge the gap from the driving range to the first tee, play more consistently, and take their game to a higher level.

-Mike Bender, March 2016-

See video for this chapter at:
http://golfs8secondsecret.com/book-chapter-videos

1

MICKELSON & WESTWOOD

THE 2013 BRITISH OPEN at Muirfield was the 62nd time Lee Westwood had competed in a major championship. At that point in his career Westwood was 0 for 62 in majors, but going into the final round at Muirfield he had a 2-stroke lead and a good chance to win. At the start of the 2015 season, only seven men had ever won their first major after their 40th birthday. Having just turned 40, Lee Westwood did not have time on his side. The weight that the Englishman was undoubtedly bearing was intensified immeasurably by the scrutiny of press around the world and specifically, the legendary British press. The *Daily Mail* wrote, "Westwood's mission today is possibly the most daunting of those met by British sportsmen this summer." *The Telegraph* added, "This [is] Westwood's day and now the world of golf will tune in to see if it is, at last, his moment." It would be difficult for him to ignore the degree of pressure from the high expectations placed on him that day, especially because this event was so close to his home country with a large crowd of United Kingdom fans watching.

Westwood had performed well in the last 20 majors, finishing in the Top 10 in half of them. For example, he was within 3 shots of the lead going into the final round in 6 of those major championships, and finished in the Top 3 eight times in majors. However, despite this high level of play, he had yet to win a big one. As of July 2013, he had won 39 professional tournaments worldwide, including two on the United States PGA Tour. He also played on eight consecutive European Ryder Cup teams, six of which were victorious. He had won the European Tour money title twice despite an international schedule. In addition, during two separate stints totaling 22 weeks during 2010 and 2011, he was the No. 1 player in the Official World Golf Ranking. By anyone's measure, he was one of the finest and most accomplished players of the early 21st century. What he seemed to be lacking in the final round of major tournaments was the ability to consistently hit the high quality shots that he exhibited in the first 3 rounds.

It was a picturesque July afternoon on the rugged Scottish links of Muirfield as Westwood began his final round of the 2013 British Open. There was no sideways rain, no flagstick-bending gales whipping off the Firth of Forth, or wind chilling temperatures to combat. Instead, occasional sun filtered through an overcast sky with a slight breeze that was just enough to make the short-sleeved golfers consult with their caddies a few moments longer than usual on strategy and club selection.

Amid these very playable conditions at Muirfield, Westwood was seeking his ever-elusive career coronation. The eyes of the golfing world were watching keenly as he negotiated the course's torturous, pot bunker-laden layout. Could he shed the label of being the "Best Player to Never Have Won a Major?"

At the start of Lee's round, BBC announcer Ken Brown intoned, "This is his biggest day in golf. He's had plenty of chances. The door is open; the door is wide open for him." The 2013 British Open was truly Westwood's moment to seize. Over the first 54 holes on an unforgiving course that had demanded his best precision and skill, Westwood had executed better than anyone else in the field and was ahead by 2 strokes.

When he arrived at the first tee box for the final round to the respectful and melodious Scottish applause, you could see his history had perhaps already gripped him. Sunglasses hid the evidence in his eyes, but his body language and nervous smile seemed to indicate that the history of being unable to close the deal was weighing on his psyche, as it should have.

Westwood took a couple of practice swings with a long-iron. As silence fell over the gallery in the surrounding bleachers, a few likely but barely discernable reasons for his failure to break through came into full focus for the world to see. First, was Westwood's inability to hit the ball in a timely fashion. That, coupled with little movement in his arms and legs, and the fact that he remained completely static for multiple seconds at address before starting his backswing may have been telling reasons for his failure to close. Given the pressures of this event, it is probable that his mental thoughts were not aligned properly for him to become champion that day.

As Westwood addressed his ball, he briefly glanced up at his intended target for a moment, and then slightly adjusted his feet. He then switched his focus to the ball for nearly 10 seconds, making only the slightest of movements in his arms and wrists. He then became virtually motionless in his feet, legs, and hips. Finally, he placed the club behind the ball at the 14-second mark (from the start of his address). From then to the subsequent takeaway 3 seconds later, there was a complete lack of visible movement. From the moment he set his feet in place, to the follow through of his arms, nearly 18 seconds had elapsed. That's far too long. This trend continued consistently for the rest of his round, and at times he took even longer to swing the club. Westwood ended up forfeiting his lead to Phil Mickelson, finishing 4 strokes back at one over par for the tournament. We believe that the debilitating effects of taking too much time and lack of movement were large contributing factors to his poor play on that final day, thus costing him the Claret Jug.

Now, let's look back for a moment to Phil Mickelson's level of play that day. His round at Muirfield was one of the greatest finishes in major tournament history. Mickelson had come from 5 shots back on that Sunday to trail by only 1 after 16 holes. Having opted not to carry a driver, he drilled his 3-wood to the center of the 17th fairway, a 578-yard par 5. From there he chose the 3-wood again, and taking no more time than with any other shot that day (about 6 seconds, while maintaining continuous movement in his legs and feet all the way up until his backswing began) he hit a laser that rolled onto the front of the green. Mickelson two-putted for birdie and went on to shoot a 66. He won by 3.

A critically important aspect of Mickelson's spectacular fourth round performance was the amount of time he spent on his shots. It took Mickelson less than 8 seconds from the moment he set his left foot in place to the completion of his follow through that led to that momentous 3-wood that found the green. This pace wasn't unique. He consistently completed his swings within 8 seconds of planting his lead foot throughout the entire round. Even as the skies clouded and the winds picked up later in the round, the amount of time it took Mickelson to hit his shots actually decreased (as brief as 6.5 to 7 seconds) throughout the day. Interestingly enough, he scored better later in the round than he did earlier, birdieing 4 of the last 6 holes. It would appear that Mickelson was in the zone in what had to be one of the most pressure filled situations in his career. Contrast Mickelson's timing with that of Lee Westwood's that day, who started with the lead but then lost it, and shot a 75. The amount of time he spent on his shots increased throughout the day, possibly contributing to his lower quality of play later in the round. From the moment his feet were planted, Westwood routinely took almost 3 times as long to hit a shot as Mickelson did, usually about 17 to 20 seconds.

Also of significant importance during the round was that before taking the club back, Mickelson moved through his address in one continuous and visible motion, which included feet, legs, hands and arms movements. By contrast, there was very limited movement in the first 14 or more seconds of Lee Westwood's address. The biggest contrast though, was Westwood's completely static posture in the last 3 seconds before starting his backswing.

Quite often, a huge problem faced by golfers of any caliber, whether they're a professional or a 20 handicapper, is that they stand at "address" too long and are lacking sufficient athletic movement. This creates tension and can 1) steal some of the feel needed for the shot, 2) tighten the swing, possibly throwing off one's rhythm and sequence, and 3) decrease the proper and necessary flow of energy. Equally important is the more time that is spent motionless, the greater the probability of negative thoughts entering the mind or other mental distractions. These distractions will affect one's confidence and mental picture (visualization) and prevent golfers from playing their best golf under the highest pressure.

> *"It's such a psychological and mental game, golf, that the smallest wrong thing at the wrong time can distract you from what you're trying to achieve."*
>
> -Lee Westwood-

Westwood's example is a bit extreme, but for most players, from beginner golfers to accomplished tour players, these dawdling and largely motionless seconds are crucial. This extra time and lack of movement allows room for mental distractions (primarily conscious thoughts) and produces tension in the muscles, leading to a restricted swing, which can result in poor shots. These are problems that this book will help train you to avoid. Many great players, players like Westwood and Garcia (especially earlier in his professional career) have problems at "address" and have not been able to wrap their hands around one of those coveted major championship trophies. Likewise, there are countless good amateur golfers around the world who can't win their club championship or state championship. While there are a myriad of reasons for this, there are two key elements that tie so many of these players together and prohibit them from achieving their highest level of play, namely 1) the inability to get through their golf swing process in a time efficient manner, and 2) not doing so in one continuously fluid motion and lacking sufficient movement. These flaws make it considerably more difficult to attain the instinctive and freer swing that is needed to perform at one's best.

To find the solution to these problems, all you need to do is recall how Phil Mickelson played that day. You can also consider the play of nearly all of the greatest golfers in history. One of the most important aspects in the development of this solution comes from studying the shot processes of the greatest major champions in golf history, the men who have each won more than five major championships. They are: Jack Nicklaus, Tiger Woods, Walter Hagen, Ben Hogan, Gary

Player, Tom Watson, Gene Sarazen, Arnold Palmer, Sam Snead, Bobby Jones, Harry Vardon, Lee Trevino, Nick Faldo, Phil Mickelson, Byron Nelson, Seve Ballesteros, James Braid, John Henry Taylor and Peter Thomson (see the total number of majors these players won on page 23). This includes Mickey Wright, Annika Sorenstam, and Juli Inkster, the women we were able to study who also won at least five majors.

We have discovered a way to duplicate this in a shot process that is made up of 3 phases. They are: **Information Gathering**, **Pre-Swing** and **Swing phases**, and the last of the two phases have 4 key elements. We call this shot process "*Golf's 8 Second Secret.*" There are many concepts and philosophies on why it's important to be confident and swing freer, and the benefits that they bring about. *Golf's 8 Second Secret* provides you with the instruction for you to bridge the gap between golf philosophy and psychology and the actions needed to be more confident and achieve a freer swing. We will guide you, step by step, through the physical and mental actions that should occur when hitting a full-swing golf shot through 3 distinct and uniquely defined phases. These phases challenge, in part, the conventional teaching ideology of how golf should be played. We use new and different terminology to make the distinction clear since some of the parts are well known while others are unique and possibly new.

The first of the three phases is one that every golfer already does to a certain extent, the **Information Gathering** phase, often referred to as the "club selection." The average 15- handicap golfer, as well as many scratch players and pros, may generally understand this phase, but too often do not perform it with enough scrutiny, and/or tend to complete it too late in the shot process. This phase requires knowledge of multiple factors. We will provide you with the fundamental information you need to know and show you how to learn, practice and experience this phase. This will give you the tools needed to train your mind to achieve increased confidence and commitment to your decision going into each shot.

Next, in the last two phases of the shot process, we completely redefine and separate the traditional "pre-shot routine" and the swing. What is commonly understood as the "pre-shot routine," we call in part, the **Pre-Swing** Phase**,** and take a whole new approach to this very important phase. The **Pre-Swing** Phase will prepare you for the Swing phase through a practice swing that merges your visualization and mental feel to obtain a physical feel. These are the two critical elements in this phase. The Pre-Swing phase will also help you move from a conscious to a more subconscious state. Phase Three, the **Swing** Phase, is the culmination of the knowledge and actions from the first two phases. It is the phase in which the mind and the body are fully integrated. As in the **Pre-Swing** Phase, it too deviates from current definitions since it combines part of the traditional "pre-shot routine" and "swing." It is time limitation and movement critical, with visualization and physical feel being key elements. Since our approach and terminology are different from traditional definitions and teachings for these two phases, we dedicate a substantial portion of Chapter 2 to making this important differentiation.

Golf's 8 Second Secret shot process will help you achieve the ultimate goal of getting you into or near the zone. When the zone is obtained, you will have even greater increased confidence and commitment, a keen and sharp focus, and more physical energy, creating better swings and shots. These attributes can build upon each other throughout the round to give you the best chance to play exceptional golf. The entire shot process covered in this book can work for all players, from neophyte competitive golfers to accomplished tour professionals looking to secure a major. Being in or near the zone will allow you to play to your highest potential with a strong competitive edge, giving you the best chance to win.

"When I play my best golf, I feel as if I'm in a fog, standing back watching the earth in orbit with a golf club in my hands."

-Mickey Wright, the winner of 13 Major Championships-

SUMMARY POINTS

- The three (3) phases of Golf's 8-second Secret are: 1) Information-Gathering phase 2) the Pre-Swing phase and 3) the Swing phase.
- There are four (4) key elements in the Pre-Swing & Swing Phases: time limitation, movement, visualization, and physical feel.
- This book redefines the traditional pre-shot routine and the swing
- Time limitation and movement are two observable traits all of golf's greatest players consistently incorporate into the pre-swing and swing phases of their shot process (with the exception of a single player on one element in one phase)
- Golf's 8 Second Secret shot process will yield freer swings, higher quality shots, more consistent play and give players the best pathway to get to the zone, where they can reach or exceed their potential.

2

A New Way to Think About the Swing

Before we dive too deep into Golf's 8 second Secret shot process, you will need to thoroughly understand the terminology and definitions of these three phases: **Information Gathering, Pre-Swing, and Swing phases.** We will also touch upon the four key elements within the last two phases. Additionally, we will contrast our shot process with the "traditional shot process" that typically includes three steps: club selection, traditional pre-shot routine, and the swing, and highlight the weak links it possesses.

PHASE ONE: INFORMATION GATHERING

The first thing a golfer must do is strategize how he or she is going to play the shot. They must evaluate many variables before choosing a final target and selecting a club. This is traditionally referred to as the "club selection". Selecting the right club is of implicit importance, there are many considerations that must be weighed in order to properly select the correct club. For example, this is where you need to analyze how the wind could affect the flight of the ball, how the lie of the ball could impact the distance and direction, and how the elevation change and topography could factor into the overall distance the ball travels both in the air and on the ground.

The current "club selection" step is loosely defined which leads to two problems. First, players tend to have insufficient knowledge. Secondly, it is quite common for golfers to blur the end of this step with the beginning of the traditional "pre-shot routine" (and at times, the swing itself). Both of these mistakes don't allow players to achieve as much confidence and commitment as they should. For this reason, we have come up with a more defined title for this critical step: the **Information Gathering phase,** or phase one in Golf's 8 Second Secret shot process. It starts when a player begins to analyze a shot to be played and ends when it's their turn to play and they've started the Pre-Swing phase. Chapter 3 will go into greater detail to give you the knowledge needed to be thorough and precise in this phase. The last two phases in Golf's 8 Second Secret shot process build upon the choices made here, so all the information needs to be well thought out and properly evaluated to create a decision with which you will be confident.

For example, take Lee Westwood again. Perhaps only having his new caddie, Mike Kerr, for about a year at the time of the 2013 Open Championship put Westwood at a slight disadvantage compared to Phil Mickelson who over the last 20 years has created an extremely strong relationship with his caddie, Bones Mackay. Experience is a key element in the Information Gathering phase, so the lack of experience shared between Westwood and Kerr could have had an effect on Westwood's game. Even many scratch players at the local and state competitive levels lack sufficient knowledge to maximize their decisions and tend to rush this phase. The key is to be as thorough and accurate as possible so you don't question your decision past this phase, unless of course, variables change. After all, the Information Gathering phase creates the base from which the rest of the shot process will be completed (which includes the swing).

Being equipped with the proper knowledge from phase one, or **Information Gathering**, will allow you to be confident and be able to commit to your **Pre-Swing** phase (which is phase two of the three phase shot process) without hard conscious thoughts about shot variables any longer, thus significantly decreasing doubt and mental distractions in the last phase, the Swing phase.

PHASE TWO: THE PRE-SWING

How the Pre-Swing Phase Differs From the Traditional Pre-Shot Routine

It is important to take note of the choice of words in this section. When we write "traditional pre-shot routine" we are referring to the traditional terminology that *starts at some point when it's a players turn to play and encompasses most, if not all, the actions and thoughts leading up to the start of the backswing.* When we write "**Pre-Swing** phase," we are referring to the second phase in Golf's 8 Second Secret shot process as described in this book. *This phase starts once a player has completed the* **Information Gathering** *phase, it's their turn to play a shot, and a trigger is initiated to start the phase. It encompasses all the actions and thoughts up until a player's lead foot is placed to start to establish their stance (address).*

Traditional pre-shot routines have been around for a long time, but they seemed to gain prominence in golf's vernacular in the 1980s when sports psychology gained popularity on the professional tours. Every player on tour now has a pre-shot routine, and so do most successful amateurs and even some higher handicap players. However, many perform the routine inconsistently or incorrectly. Former PGA tour winner and current NBC golf analyst Roger Maltbie once said of the pre-shot routine, "It creates habit, it creates routine. If the body and mind do the same thing all the time, they should be able to do it whether it's in a pressure situation or not." In other words, its purpose is to condition you to become consistent each time you swing the club.

Nowadays, most every accomplished player, sports psychologist, instructor and PGA Professional agrees that the pre-shot routine is necessary and important. So what exactly is a pre-shot routine? We know this seems elementary, but stick with us here.

Normally, the pre-shot routine has been defined as a series of actions, thoughts, and behaviors that are performed systematically and consistently before the swing starts (meaning before the backswing starts). Its purpose is primarily to set up the mind and body for maximum performance. Most, if not all, sports psychologists recommend using pre-shot routines.

The amount of time spent during the traditional pre-shot routine often varies as much as the routines themselves. Some players perform quick and simple pre-shot routines, while others turn the pre-shot routine into a laborious grind that kills the pace of play and hinders their performance, especially under pressure. Contrary to popular belief, renowned sports psychologists Bob Rotella, Richard Coop, and most of their brethren, do not teach clients to spend more time over the ball or to play the game deliberately slow. The basis of their methodology is that you need to find a *consistently repetitive* way of making sure you are as prepared as you can possibly be to play each shot. Rotella wrote in his book, *Golf Is Not A Game of Perfect,* "To score more consistently, a golfer must think consistently. A sound, consistent pre-shot routine makes it easier." Nowhere does he say that it should be a long, laborious process, and we agree with this philosophy. In fact, USGA rule 6-7 dictates that a shot must be played "without undue delay," and allows committees to regulate this time, which usually can't exceed 40 seconds per shot, barring special conditions. That doesn't leave time for a long drawn out pre-shot routine. We would never counsel a golfer to swing the club before they are ready, but the problem is that too many players simply take too long in their pre-shot routines. This leaves time for both mental distractions and physical tension to build up and carry over to the swing, likely leading to poorer quality shots and inconsistent golf. Additionally, some players fail to spend enough time in the pre-shot routine. This leads to insufficient mental and physical preparation which can cause problems in the swing phase.

How long should the Pre-Shot routine be?

Based on our study of golf's greatest players, we found that there is a correlation between the amount of time spent in traditional pre-shot routines and a golfer's ability to execute consistent high-quality shots and play well under pressure. The goal for any golfer should be to create a balance between reaping the benefits of a good pre-shot routine without rushing it, and not leaving too much room for distraction and stiffness to enter the equation. To do that, there needs to be a distinct starting and stopping point for one's routine that will help ensure that timing and movements are consistent. So when should the pre-shot routine begin, and when should it end?

Some players say that their pre-shot routine begins when they grab their club from their bag. Others say it's at the beginning of their practice swing(s) after they've teed up the ball, and even others believe it begins when they begin to address the ball. In reality, a golfer's pre-shot routine could begin anywhere since it's their own personal routine. We see this as a mistake. Since there is no clear-cut starting point, a blurred line is created that fails to differentiate the traditional club selection step from the pre-shot routine. Additionally, it is pretty much universally believed that the pre-shot routine ends when the backswing begins, another point with which we disagree.

The mind is very involved during the pre-shot routine. Acclaimed golf psychologist, Joseph Parent, in his book, *Zen Golf: Mastering the Mental Game,* described the proper mindset when he said, "The ideal state of mind for the action is feeling confident, focused, and in the flow, with body and mind synchronized in the present moment." Following the traditional shot process, some of the correct physical actions may be happening in the pre-shot routine but the mind might not be up to speed with the body. It may still be thinking about variables from the club selection step when it is supposed to be visualizing the ensuing shot and developing feel for the swing. If there is no set starting point to the pre-shot; if there is lack of a disciplined routine; if one has not yet made a committed decision; gray areas are created that the brain has to unnecessarily negotiate through. The more time the brain spends sorting out information during the pre-shot routine, the less time the golfer has to narrow his or her focus, visualize the shot, and gain feel for the swing. Doubt and other mental distractions can begin to creep in, which can wreak havoc on decisions that were previously made about strategy. All thoughts may be jumbled together, especially if too much time is spent in the pre-shot routine. To add to this hesitation, if the golfer is lacking sufficient movement, physical repercussions can have an effect on the fluidity of the swing. As we all know, confidence and unrestricted free movements are key in golf. Therefore, tense muscles and a weakly committed or distracted mindset can significantly hinder one's performance.

Most of today's golf instruction is centered around improving one's technical skills by working primarily on the mechanics of the full swing. Improving one's swing is extremely important but will only take a player so far. Instructors very often leave out talking about a traditional pre-shot routine until players are more advanced in their skill levels. Even then, much of the time, the details of exactly what to do can be vague and not well defined. In our opinion, this very important area of the game is grossly under taught. No matter how good a swing technically becomes, it will not perform as well as it could without a solid pre-shot routine. A strong pre-shot routine within one's shot process is a key component needed for consistent results.

Our Definition of Pre-Swing Phase
VS.
Traditional Pre-Shot Routine

It has been proven to us, over and over, that the traditional "pre-shot routine" and "swing" combination does not consistently deliver on its intended goal. After analyzing and understanding the traditional pre-shot routine, we realized that there was a better and clearer method to make it easier to decrease tension, mental distractions, and create a stronger feel. The brain likes continuous and consistently sound thoughts, which is why we developed the three phases in Golf's 8 Second Secret in the way that we did, to teach you that the brain and the body can progress from one phase to the next uninhibited. This is most evident in Golf's 8 Second Secret's **Pre-Swing phase,** where golfers can progress from this second phase, to the **Swing Phase,** without the debilitating break that is customary between the traditional pre-shot routine and the actual start of the backswing. The stop and start between different thoughts and actions can cause distraction and confusion at an awkward time. Also, during this phase, the body should never be completely stagnant. There should always be some movement, even as small as one's fingers massaging the grip and/or slight movements of the feet.

If a golfer can focus all of his or her attention on one phase at a time, decidedly perform it, and then move on to the next phase, they are less likely to question their decisions and actions. This strongly reduces the possibility of doubt and increases confidence and leads to stronger commitment for the Swing phase. These ideas were the basis behind developing the new definition of this second phase, named, the **Pre-Swing** phase.

To combat some of the problems that were discussed regarding the traditional "pre-shot routine," we have come to define Golf's 8 Second Secret **Pre-Swing phase** as starting upon successful completion of the Information Gathering phase, it's your turn to play and you've initiated your trigger (as discussed later in the book). This needs to be a very clear and distinct starting point so *the mind knows that it can trust its previous decisions*, and is no longer thinking consciously about shot variables. Remember, a common fault with the traditional pre-shot routine is that very often a golfer will still be thinking about shot variables from the traditional club selection step. Additionally, the pre-shot routine's end point is when the takeaway for the backswing begins. We Define the end of Golf's 8 Second Secret Pre-Swing phase as being when your right foot (for right handed players) is about to be planted to start to establish the stance (more on this in a moment).

Since taking too long to prepare for the shot can create a host of issues in this phase, time is critically important. As such, instead of having an undefined allotment of time for the pre-swing phase, we have limited the amount of time needed to complete this phase. We will break down the timing aspect in greater detail in Chapter 4 and layout exactly what needs to occur in our Pre-Swing phase, but for now just recognize that there is a time limitation. Stemming from this, at no point during our Pre-Swing phase will you be completely motionless, thereby combating the possibility of becoming stiff, allowing muscles to tighten and feel to diminish. Again, movements here can be very slight, such as re-gripping the club with your fingers, and or feet movements. The main objective of the Pre-Swing phase is to rehearse the swing to be executed, where you will marry your mind to your muscles by merging the visualization with your mental feel to obtain your physical feel through a practice swing(s).

PHASE THREE: THE SWING

All golf instruction, including lessons, books, magazine articles, and DVDs, inevitably treat the golf swing as beginning with "the backswing." A television analyst that uses ultra-slow-speed footage to analyze a tour professional's swing starts with the set-up position just before takeaway. In book or magazine swing sequences, what do we see in the first frame; the set-up position, right? Instructors typically teach you only the golf mechanics that occur at set-up and from the time the backswing starts through to the follow through. Thus, everyone thinks that's where the swing starts, and that's what is taught.

Wrong!

*We have redefined the **Swing (swing phase)** as starting when the lead foot (right foot for right handed players) is being moved into place to establish your stance (address) and is complete at the end of the follow through.* It is this *placing of the right foot*, then the left, and then a final adjustment with the right, that helps to continue the positive movement and energy flow that started in our Pre-Swing phase. This movement continues throughout your feet, legs, hands and arms. This "energizing" will carry you through to the backswing and follow through. This starting point for Golf's 8 Second Secret **Swing phase** deviates significantly from common concepts and teachings.

To reiterate, we believe that one of the biggest weaknesses with the traditional shot process is that there is a clear-cut break between the end of the traditional "pre-shot routine" and the start of the "traditional swing" (the backswing), making the transition to the backswing more difficult than it needs to be. This break, which most golfers have, affects both the mind and the body in three ways. First, the break inhibits the brain's thought process from translating the results of the "pre-shot routine" to the final execution of the swing as effectively as possible. Secondly, the break will also physically affect you in that it can diminish or hinder the energy generated to that point. Thirdly, the physical feel that you have established to this point can be impaired.

Newton's First Law states, "An object in motion tends to stay in motion, while an object at rest tends to stay at rest." From this, we might conclude that the stop and start, or break, caused by the traditional definitions and teachings of the "pre-shot" and "swing" combination creates a barrier to the continuous and fluid motion needed for a consistently strong swing. We almost called this book, *Your Swing Starts Here,* to underscore this very important point.

A New Way to Think About the Swing

Building off of this, while shot visualization and a strong physical feel are two elements of our Swing phase, the two most critical elements of this phase are the time spent in the phase and continuous and rhythmic movement. As a whole, these two critical elements are often undervalued. We will be stressing the significance of these two elements in greater detail in Chapters 4 & 5, but for now, recognize that our **Swing phase** is not open-ended with regard to time, and continuous movement is critical.

These new definitions are more than just semantics. The real evidence for defining the pre-swing and swing this way comes from the great players themselves.

The table on the following page identifies those elite players of the game who have won five or more majors. We believe they knew or at least subconsciously sensed our definition of when the swing begins. It has everything to do with how much time they took and what movements they made and were able to repeat from one swing to the next. Study their swings and you'll find that they are repetitive *to within a second or so* from the moment that their lead foot is placed. (Nicklaus is the only substantial exception. See Chapter 5 for the explanation.) This means that even if these players made this delineation subconsciously, they knew that their swing motion began earlier than today's definition of when the swing starts.

Please visit our website: (**www.Golfs8SecondSecret.com**) where you can click on links to view video footage of some of the greats' Information Gathering phase, with many performing the Pre-Swing phase and most of them performing the Swing phase, along with other video related to the book. You will be able to see the similarities in the timing and movements of their swing phase.

Rank	Golfer	Number of Majors Won
1	Jack Nicklaus	18
2	Tiger Woods	14
3	Walter Hagen	11
T4	Ben Hogan	9
T4	Gary Player	9
6	Tom Watson	8
T7	Gene Sarazen	7
T7	Arnold Palmer	7
T7	Sam Snead	7
T7	Bobby Jones	7
T7	Harry Vardon	7
T12	Lee Trevino	6
T12	Nick Faldo	6
T14	Phil Mickelson	5
T14	Byron Nelson	5
T14	Seve Ballesteros	5
T14	James Braid	5
T14	John Henry Taylor	5
T14	Peter Thomson	5

Coaches, teachers and even players themselves, have talked *around* this subject for decades. Even Ben Hogan seemed to allude to this same idea in his timeless book, *Five Lessons - The Modern Fundamentals of Golf,* but did not explicitly state it as we are doing here. In Chapter 3 of his book, which is titled "**The First Part Of The Swing,**" he begins the first *four pages* talking about the waggle, an event that occurs *before* the actual backswing begins. Following current ideology, this step would be typically classified within the realm of the traditional "pre-shot routine" but Hogan decidedly chose to put it in his, **"The First Part of the Swing"** section instead. Thus, he *knew,* to some degree, that the takeaway was NOT the first step of the swing. One of the game's earliest and respected teachers, Seymour Dunn, also touched upon this, but to our knowledge no one today has addressed this concept directly.

This may not be so hard to digest if you consider examples from other sports. Take baseball for example. Does the pitcher's motion begin when he draws his arm back before the forward motion and release? Not really. It begins once his dominant foot is in place and he leans forward, having received the sign from the catcher. He *then* pulls his upper body back up to start his "wind-up." The movements and thoughts leading up to the wind-up are an *important* part of his throw. It is in these moments where his thoughts become properly aligned and his body is sufficiently energized. As a result, any pitcher working to improve his pitching motion starts there, with setting up his body properly to make sure everything is in place for the ensuing action. His motion does not begin with the isolated drawing back of the ball before the throw. As golfers, this same strategy can be applied to our own efforts to increase performance.

Next, consider Rafael Nadal's serve in tennis. Would you say it begins when he throws the ball up high into the air and lifts to his toes to jump? Of course not. His serving routine begins once his feet are being placed, followed by a few bounces of the ball. Only then does he toss the ball in the air and jump to hit it. He performs the same movements every time.

In basketball, does a foul shot begin when the player lifts the ball just before they release it? No. It typically starts with the placement of his or her feet and a flex in the knees. Then most players will dribble the ball, and shift it to their shooting hand, securing the feel they need for the shot just as accomplished golfers do with the waggle.

The most important issue to note here is that, in any of these sports and many others, the "swing" equivalent begins with the placing of the feet. This begins a brief, consistent, and precise routine that starts to energize the body. It is always the same, never changing, thus creating consistent results. We're convinced that great athletes in all sports instinctively know how important these seconds and movements leading up to the action of performance are, whether consciously or not. We're positive they would agree that, whatever sport they're playing, the equivalent Swing Phase typically begins with the lead foot being placed. So wouldn't it make sense for a golf swing to also start at that point?

DECLINE OF FEEL IN TODAY'S MODERN GOLF

We're sure you've heard the saying "golf is a game of feel" countless times. We see it as an important component of executing your best golf, but what does it mean? There are two different "types" of feel: mental feel and physical feel. The dynamic between the two is interesting because both types need to be equally strong in order to perform your best golf. Many players nowadays, however, are severely lacking the necessary mental feel. Simply put, we define mental feel as the ability to evaluate a golf situation based on variables (i.e. yardage), experience and instinct. Physical feel, on the other hand is the translation of mental feel into a certain physical action. Together they enable you to use finesse when controlling your swing. These ideas are a bit abstract because they are difficult to describe explicitly. The following history of yardage evaluation tools, or yardage aids may help to illustrate the concept and also explain the recent decline of feel in modern golf.

It is generally accepted that modern golf originated in Scotland and gained popularity in Britain and parts of Europe in the late 19th century. On these original courses and even internationally in the United States up to about the 1950's and early '60's there were rarely yardage markers on courses. That's right, not even a 150-yard marker! Players typically had next to no idea how far away from the hole they were. Having no yardage markers, they had to rely on instinct. Golfers had to learn through experience to develop the ability to accurately judge shot distance. Consequently, mental feel was crucial to performing well. As a result, golf became a "game of feel." It has been said that some of the best golfers in the 1940's and '50's, such as Ben Hogan, when driving from course-to-course, would replay shots in their head to train their minds to evaluate yardage without any additional aids. Both historical and modern accounts of people that play or grew up playing solely using their own judgment for distance assert that playing like this helps a golfer to rely more heavily on **all of their senses**. Over time, through trial and error and constant growth from experience, the best golfers became more confident in their abilities, which prompted a more committed swing. In fact, it wasn't until 1961 that Jack Nicklaus used yardage books that he compiled by pacing off entire golf courses. He is one of the first to be credited with winning an important championship (the 1961 U.S. Amateur) through the use of a yardage book. Then he was the first professional to win a Major (at the 1962 U.S Open at Oakmont) by doing so. It wasn't until the mid 1960's and 1970's that rudimentary 100, 150 and 200-yard markers became the norm on golf courses. In the '80's, golf courses began marking their sprinkler heads with exact distances, and in the mid '90's precise digital measuring devices, such as laser range finders were introduced and became commonplace. Since then, there has been a systematic degradation in the need for a golfer to use his or her own judgment in determining distance. As a result, there has been a diminishing of the senses that are needed for obtaining a sharp mental and physical feel.

Granted, the art of feel isn't entirely lost because it is still very important in the short game. You never see someone "laser" the distance of a putt or pitches within 25 yards. Most players judge the speed or strength of a chip shot solely by mental feel and translate it into physical feel or "touch". In terms of full swing golf shots, whether you realize it or not, mental feel is still a critical component. You may use a range finder, yardage book, or the knowledge of a caddie to help you select a club, but when it comes time to commit to a shot and take your last look at the pin (or whatever your target is) it is "feel" that signals your brain to tell your muscles how fast to swing the club: soft, medium or hard. Your brain and body instinctively synchronize in those moments to hopefully produce the result you envision. Therefore, it can be postulated that once you have selected a club that will get the ball to your target area, say within a 2 or 3 yard circle, your feel may get you even closer to the target area. Knowing the exact net yardage is helpful, but it is not the sole controlling element when it comes to execution. Having a strong feel allows you to correctly factor in the effects of wind, lie of the ball, and elevation change, amongst other variables. In truth, yardage aids, to some degree, may give you a false sense of confidence for the variables that affect the "true" yardage. So following this logic, you can increase your accuracy and the overall quality of your shots by training your mind to utilize feel and to play more instinctively.

There is a theory that the East Course at the legendary Merion Golf Club in Ardmore, Pennsylvania, is trying to get golfers to go back to the roots of golf and play solely with feel. Its use of the signature wicker baskets on the pin sticks instead of flags, the complete lack of yardage markers, and the ban on range finders, brings back feel as an essential part of the game. A possible reason for using baskets instead of flags is to eliminate any information that one could gather pertaining to wind direction and strength, by which way a flag blows. This mimics some original courses in Scotland, dating as far back as the 1800's, thus forcing one to rely more heavily on analytical thinking and instinctive decision making. Others theorize that the baskets were better equipped to handle the wind on a links course. Either way, they make the player rely more heavily on feel and instinct.

Inevitably, there will be situations when you will be unable to get an accurate distance number. For example, when you're laying up to a creek or pond and want to be short of either, or when you hit a shot far to the left or right and the angle with obstacles (i.e. trees) makes it difficult to determine the exact yardage. Those playing on professional tours are not typically allowed to use range finders in competition, nor would it be totally beneficial to do so given our theory on feel. The fact of the matter is that even range finders are not the be-all and end-all. You need feel to be able to properly assess *all* of the variables that could affect your shot, not just distance, i.e. elevation change, firmness of the greens, etc. Without distance aids you would have to base your decision solely on judgment and if your skills are not finely tuned you may leave the shot considerably short or hit it long. Additionally, if you are questioning your abilities, self-doubt could be introduced and negatively affect your swing. This tends to happen most often under pressure because your "feel abilities" are not as strongly trained as your physical swing. Either way, your shot doesn't end up where you want it to go.

> *"There is no such thing as natural touch. Touch is something you create by hitting millions of golf balls."*
> *-Lee Trevino-*

As further evidence for how important feel is, let's consider Ben Hogan again. He is universally known to be one of the best ball strikers ever, but mechanically speaking, his swing was by no means perfect. Was it feel that gave him that extra edge? If you look at the younger modern players today who have trained tirelessly with the world's best swing coaches, many of their physical swings couldn't be any more perfect, yet there are few, if any, Ben Hogan's. If you placed a technically sound player next to Ben Hogan on a practice range, I'm sure they would both hit fantastic shots consistently. However, many of today's technically sound players will struggle to transfer those same results onto the golf course, whereas Hogan would be able to perform equally well on both the practice tee and the course. Why can't so many young players transfer their skills from the practice tee to the course? And what sets Hogan and golf's elite players, both professionals and amateurs alike, above the others?

It is impossible for us to know precisely what is going on in these golfers' minds since it's difficult to measure mental and physical feel. Yet the history and origin of golf as a whole, combined with trends observed in modern players who seem to lack the feel of a Ben Hogan would indicate that feel is an intrinsic element of great championship golf.

HOW DOES ALL OF THIS FIT IN WITH THE SHOT PROCESS?

In Ancient Egypt, scribes used to look at marks on the banks of the Nile River to see how high the river was capable of rising and used this as an estimate to safeguard against floods. What would happen if an unexpectedly heavy rainstorm upstream caused the river to rise above those telltale marks? Cities or towns would be damaged of course. Most golfers have only prepared their mechanical swing and mental game to withstand a certain amount of pressure. What is likely to happen when they encounter a situation in which pressures exceeds what they encounter during practice or typical day-to-day golf? A flood of woe, that's what.

One of the goals of this book is to teach you how to utilize and strengthen feel as an added tool in your repertoire (shot process). This is essential to all stock shots, unique shot circumstances and high-pressure situations. We all understand the importance of having feel but for many of today's golfers, it is a mystery how to train and harness that skill. Training to gain a stronger mental feel and thus physical feel for your shots in the Pre-Swing and Swing Phases will likely benefit your entire game.

In the end, what you are trying to achieve is to have every swing be equally strong. Whether it's a driver on the first hole of a friendly weekend round or a 5-iron for your second shot on the 72nd hole at Augusta National when a par would win the Masters by 1 stroke, a strong feel is critical.

PRESSURE!

Every amateur golfer, no matter their experience, will face a situation in which their pressure threshold will be tested. For a less experienced golfer it may be a round of limited consequence when a small amount of pressure is applied while playing a $5 Nassau with a friend. For a more competitive player it may be a tournament stroke-play qualifier or a round that determines whether a cut is made to advance to match play in a tournament. Finally, for the most advanced golfer, it may be the last 9 holes of a tournament in which there is a chance to win one of your biggest tournaments.

For tour professionals this pressure is of the same intensity but occurs at different levels. For example, a young professional's threshold may occur when he or she is in the lead going into the final round of a tournament. For seasoned professionals it may occur during a major. Lee Westwood has won more than 40 times around the world; he has proven that he can handle the pressure of a European Tour or PGA Tour event. However, he has never won a major. Undoubtedly, the pressure he feels in a major is significantly more intense than during those regular Tour events, and that pressure appears to be a tipping point that tests his game and his swing to a higher degree.

It may seem as if we are picking on Westwood here but he is not alone. There are many Tour players that are successful but can't seem to win a major and many more still who have been playing for years but struggle to win regular season events. These shortcomings may result from a flawed shot process that cannot handle these moments of extra pressure.

Whatever your pressure "ceiling" is, Golf's 8 Second Secret will help. It is designed to expand your confidence and comfort zones, thereby freeing up your swing. Now that we have introduced the concept of Golf's 8-Second Secret you are ready to tackle Phase One in the next chapter.

SUMMARY POINTS

- In the Information Gathering phase you will examine all aspects of the golf shot to come to a decisive conclusion. There should be little to no possibility of questioning your decisions as you move into Phase Two, the Pre-Swing. The Information Gathering phase is when confidence and commitment first come into play. There is no time constraint here, though you should aim to be time efficient. It starts when a player begins to analyze a shot to be played and ends when it's their turn to play and they've started the Pre-Swing phase.
- Golf's 8 Second Secret redefines the traditional pre-shot routine and swing into the Pre-Swing and Swing phases, whose starting and ending points are different and unique.
- The Pre-Swing phase starts when it's a players turn to play and a trigger is initiated. It ends when the lead foot is first placed to establish the swing stance. The Pre-Swing phase is time limited and contains a flow of movements designed to energize and create feel. You merge your visualization with your mental feel to obtain a physical feel.
- The new start and stop points of the Pre-Swing phase and Swing phase eliminate the break found in the traditional shot process, pre-shot routine and swing.
- The Swing Phase starts with the lead foot being moved into place to start to establish your stance and ends with the follow through. It is strictly time limited and movement filled and the visualization and physical feel are carried over from the Pre-Swing Phase.
- Visualization is having a mental picture or imagery of seeing the flight path of the ball flying to the target.

- Mental Feel is the ability to evaluate a golf shot based on intuition gained through knowledge and experience.
- Physical Feel is the transfer of mental feel into physical action, where you seem to sense the correct ensuing actions of performance throughout your body and in your muscles.
- Both types of feel are necessary to perform your best golf, though mental feel has been systematically degraded as golf has become more modern.
- The key elements within the shot process: time limitation, movement, visualization and feel, are designed to act as a catalyst to move your mind from conscious thoughts and actions to primarily subconscious thoughts and actions, leading to more instinctive and freer swings.

3

INFORMATION GATHERING (PHASE ONE)

"Confidence in golf means being able to concentrate on the problem at hand with no outside interference."

-Tom Watson-

THE INFORMATION GATHERING PHASE is the first phase in the shot process. It is arguably the most undervalued phase in golf. If the information that is accumulated in this phase is accurate and sound, it will increase your confidence and commitment, having a very positive effect on your swing and shot.

Essentially, this phase creates the base for the rest of the shot process. This has traditionally been referred to as the "club selection routine". If you frequently make miscalculations in this phase and thus tend to misjudge your distances, during a windy day for example, play can get frustrating and negatively influence your mental focus, decision-making, and patience. This affects your score accordingly. In order to execute one's best swings and shots, golfers have to consistently study, practice and experience the variables in order to keep mentally tuned up. The Information Gathering phase is where golfers obtain knowledge, mental feel, and initial visualization so that they are confident and committed going into the Pre-Swing phase.

TROUBLE ON THE 12TH

To illustrate how important this phase is, let's take a look at PGA Tour star Jordan Spieth's performance in the final round of the 2014 Masters. Spieth provided a classic example of how not having the proper information, knowledge, and mental feel could play a role in victory or defeat.

In 2013, at the age of 19, Spieth became the youngest PGA Tour winner in 82 years when he captured the John Deere Classic. Having turned 20 by the time he arrived at Augusta for the 2014 Masters, he played well beyond his years and became the youngest 54-hole leader in Masters history. After Spieth birdied four of the first seven holes on Sunday, he led the tournament by two strokes and had an excellent chance to win the green jacket, which would have displaced Tiger Woods as the youngest champion. Instead, during the middle of his round, he made some critical mistakes in the Information Gathering phase which may have contributed to his downfall and allowed Bubba Watson to win the championship for the second time in three years. We believe the biggest momentum changer for Spieth was at the 570-yard par-5 8th hole. He played a smart tee shot, hitting a well placed 3-wood to take the two bunkers on the right out of play. Spieth pushed his second shot a bit to the right of the green, but if anything, that was a good place to miss. This left him with a pitch shot that wasn't too difficult, for he had ample green to work with. He still had an excellent chance for birdie, and it seemed the worst he'd make was par. It was here that everything seemed to go awry. Spieth and his caddie, Michael Greller, discussed where to land the ball on the green, but they apparently miscalculated how much the ball would release due to the lie of the ball in the grass, and the shot stopped about 30 feet short and left of the pin. Spieth proceeded to hit a poor first putt, then missed a four-footer for par, both admittedly misreads. His bogey, coupled with Watson's birdie on the hole, erased Spieth's lead.

At the 460-yard par-4 9th hole, Spieth was in the middle of the fairway, 151 yards from the pin, in perfect position to hit a high quality shot to give himself a good chance at birdie. Instead, he made bogey. He said he slightly mishit his approach but the problem was more likely that he didn't give himself enough room for error on the shot as most experienced Masters winners would have. Had he been more experienced, he would have realized that it was better to miss a bit long rather than pin high or just short. It appears that he didn't have enough club (that would have given him room for a slight mishit) for a shot that has forever tricked even experienced players, let alone the 20-year-old first-timer. The false front of the green helps create an illusion that the hole is closer than it really is (knowledge and feel). Spieth's approach landed on the false front and rolled back down the hill onto the fairway. He failed to get up and down for par and Watson birdied again. Spieth suddenly found himself two shots behind and wobbling after a four-shot swing in the span of about 20 minutes.

Any chance Spieth had of recovering died in Rae's Creek on the devilish 12th hole often referred to as one of the trickiest par-3s in golf. Greller told Spieth it was 149 gross yards to the hole and 141 to safely clear the bank in front of the green on the line he was taking to the pin. All day, players had been gauging the pin at 153 gross yards, meaning a 145-yard carry to the front of the green. Spieth hit the shot he thought he needed to hit, but due to the incorrect information, the ball landed on the bank between the green and the creek, and tumbled back into the water, leading to a good bogey but keeping him 2 shots back.

Having the correct information on a consistent basis helps to develop one's mental feel. This is critical in this very precise and fickle game, and it takes accrued experience to excel. One of the goals of this chapter is to provide you with the information-gathering skills you need to be able to correctly plan for an upcoming shot. During this phase you will formulate a plan and commit to it, as illustrated in the aforementioned Spieth narrative, familiarity with the course will greatly aid you during the Information Gathering phase. *The more you know the course, the details (i.e. slopes, elevation changes, etc.) of the holes and greens, the more confident, committed and instinctive you can be as you play your round. This is why most players perform better on their home course.*

THE INFORMATION GATHERING PHASE

The main parts of this phase are as follows: 1) Determining the target (area), distance needed to be played, and analyzing all the variables that could affect one's shot (wind, elevation change, lie of the ball, etc.) 2) Choosing the flight path (visualization starts), type of shot (stock shot or unique shot, i.e. draw, fade, punch shot, etc.), and club to be played (these can occur in a different order in your mind i.e. the chicken or the egg scenario) 3) the natural progression of starting to acquire both a mental and physical feel for the shot.

The information in this chapter is designed to 1) equip you with the knowledge needed to properly evaluate each shot and 2) stress the importance of remembering your past experience of both shot and course conditions. This will help you to build a strong library of knowledge and secure a consistently strong mental feel, 3) enable you to walk away with a confident decision and commitment to the shot.

Information Gathering (Phase One)

There are no exact formulas to determine how variables will affect the ball, but there are general guidelines. As such, it is of great importance that you continually practice them and gain experience in order to produce the best shots possible.

In this chapter, we will break down the different aspects that can affect a shot such as: wind (more times than not the most important variable); shot elevation change; lie of the ball; conditions of grass, fairways, and greens; temperature; and course altitude. Then, once you have this information, we will take you through the general thinking process that occurs by using an example from one of golf's most iconic holes, Number 12, the par-3, at Augusta National.

It's important to say from the start that a time constraint does not apply to the Information Gathering phase. The fact is, shot conditions, from wind, to elevation change, to the lie of the ball, etc., vary greatly from shot to shot. A 170-yard shot from the fairway on a calm day under ideal conditions, with no hazards, may not require much deliberation. A shot of the same distance on a side-hill lie from difficult rough with a swirling wind on a 55-degree day, with a creek just left of the green, will require much more consideration. This is where mental feel is most important in a strong shot process. Therefore, the Information Gathering phase theoretically does not have a set time limit. As stated in the previous chapter, and we will reiterate here, it is still important to be time efficient in this phase to maintain the pace of play and a sense of athleticism. As you practice and learn this phase, becoming more experienced and comfortable with it, the amount of time it takes for you to evaluate a shot, along with the variables that could affect your shot will decrease. If you take too long or are indecisive, then an important athletic type of flow and rhythm could be compromised. In an effort to be timely, some of the factors can be analyzed well before you get to your ball, and certain elements, such as the forecasted wind speed and direction, temperature and course altitude can be somewhat evaluated even before you play your first tee shot. *What's most critical here is that you review all the variables that might affect your swing and shot, then make a decision that you will not second guess, thus giving you confidence and commitment going into the pre-swing phase.*

Establishing Your Club Distances

One of the first things you must do early in the season and during the season as needed, is determine a baseline for yourself with regard to how far you hit each of your clubs in calm and average temperature conditions. These measurements are very important to everything you are about to learn. There are two ways of determining how far you hit your shots. The first is to find a fairly flat fairway or patch of land and hit 5 shots with each club (hit #1 balls with your PW, #2s with your 9 and, #3s with your 8 for example), walk to the groupings and with a rangefinder sight the distances back to your golf bag next to the area from where you hit. Do this for each of your clubs and record the distances. The important thing here is for you to come away with the knowledge for how far your shots carried. Your roll out will vary from course to course and day to day based on the variables, i.e. ground firmness, etc.. You'll need to make adjustments accordingly. The second way for you to establish how far you hit your clubs is to contact a professional with access to a launch monitor. They'll be able to use the monitor to help you accurately determine your carry distance for each club. The distances obtained with your irons (for men) should be approximately 8 to 12 yards apart from each other. The spread between each club is more for longer hitters. If you find that your club's distances don't follow this trend, then it's possible that one or more of your lofts are off and you should be able to get them adjusted.

Remember, sometimes even just a couple of yards difference could spell trouble for a given shot. Another thing you should note while establishing your baseline is to determine a reasonable run out from certain clubs such as hybrids, fairway metals, and your driver. It's important to know both the carry on these shots, in case there is an obstacle or hazard your ball must carry, and the run out once the ball lands.

Armed with your numbers and confident with a solid base, you can apply this knowledge to the calculations you will need to make on the golf course.

PRE-ROUND ANALYSIS – DAY OF

Wind, temperature, and course altitude are factors that can be partially or fully analyzed *before you tee off* on the first hole. Knowing this information (check your weather app) before you get to the course will help you stay more consistent throughout the round and will leave you with less to think about.

Wind

Wind is unique in that you should not only check it before the round but also throughout the round as well since it will affect each shot differently. In terms of pre-round analysis, you should check the forecast for wind before you get to the course. Take note of its overall direction, speed, and any predicted changes along with the estimated times for the changes throughout the day. Sometimes it can be calm early on and pick up considerably later on, especially if there is also an expected temperature change. One good tip once you know this information and get to the course is to mark up your scorecard. Draw an arrow on the course map (if available) indicating the direction of the prevailing wind, its speed, any estimated speed and directional changes, and anticipated time of these changes to use as an added reference.

Temperature

Temperature is a good thing to note about 1 hour before the round because you won't have a way to check it throughout the course of play (you'll just need to feel it). Overall, when the mercury is on the rise, the golf ball becomes softer and more easily compressed. Therefore it will catapult faster off the face of the club creating more velocity, resulting in a longer distance. When the ball lands, it will typically have more bounce, which will give you more yards on the run out. On a colder day, the air density is heavier and the ball simply doesn't travel as far because there isn't as much compression, velocity, and spin.

Also, hotter air is lighter air, and the hotter the temperature the less drag and lift your shots will have. Trajectory is lower as temperature rises, so slices and hooks are minimized. Let's say your base temperature is 70 when you establish club distances. You know how far you hit each of your irons at that temperature. An average player may add a half club, plus or minus, for each 10 degrees below that temperature, or subtract a half club, plus or minus, for each 10-degree increment above it. A good rule of thumb is that a 10-degree increase or decrease in temperature adds or subtracts the equivalent of 2 to 3 yards to be played (more for longer hitters). Here, your greatest knowledge will come from experience and memory, which develops your mental feel.

Temperature is something you can begin to keep track of the night before and then recheck the morning of the round. Normally the temperature will be predicted to increase during the day, so note what those numbers are during the time of your round. You (or your caddie) will keep that in mind as your round progresses, noting how far shots are carrying. For example, if you are starting early in the morning, it is quite typical that the temperature could rise from 60 degrees to 80 degrees during your round, which could create an approximately 5 to 6 yard increase in distance for each shot.

Course Altitude

If you are playing at a course at which the altitude is considerably different than your home course, then it's important to take note of this and adjust shot distances. A general rule is:

- *The ball travels 1 percent farther for every additional 500 feet of elevation above sea level.*

You should note that this has more of an effect on short irons than long irons due to the typical higher ball flight.

- *For SW (sand wedge) through 7-iron, distance will change by slightly more than 1%, 1% for 6-iron through 4-iron, and slightly less than 1% for everything below that.*

For example: In West Palm Beach a 7-iron might travel 150 yards. In Chicago, at approximately 600 feet above sea level, the same shot will travel say 1.2 percent, or 1.8 yards farther. In Denver, at approximately 5,500 feet, that 7-iron shot will carry 11 percent or 16.5 yards farther. If you are playing somewhere with an elevation different than what you are used to, then it is important to go to the driving range before the round and see just how much of an effect it has on your ball.

IN ROUND ANALYSIS

Target Determination

The first thing you must do to analyze any shot is choose a target, or more specifically, a target area where you want your ball to end up. Secondly, calculate the *gross yardage* and analyze a number of variables to obtain the *net yardage*. When choosing a target, the key factor is one's accessibility to an ideal target area which typically comes down to a choice between risk versus reward based on obstacles and hazards to and through your target area. For example, bunkers, water hazards, high rough, etc. and their proximity to your target area and the club you plan to use. Simultaneously, you must analyze other variables, which will be discussed in more detail, and the effect or possible effect they'll have on your shot. *As a general guideline, your goal is to pick a target (area) that will produce the optimum result based on your skill level, distance from the target, variables, any obstacles and hazards that exist through your intended flight path and roll out, and how confident and committed you'll be to the shot.* A rule of thumb is that your target area should be to the side of the pin, fairway, or lay-up area opposite, long, or short of the obstacles and hazards that pose the greatest risk, or to put it differently, you should be picking an area that allows for the greatest margin of error while still achieving your objective for the shot, hole and round. There are many factors and variables to consider. This book can by no means address every type of scenario. As circumstances on the golf course change, many stock and situational shots will arise that will test a golfers' knowledge and experience. This is fundamentally crucial to one achieving their best shots and swings.

When choosing a target, it is crucially important for you to pick a very tight, very small target area. This is the earliest stage where you begin to focus your mind and start to develop mental feel for the ensuing shot. Once you've chosen your target, it is our belief that from a pitching wedge or less, your goal should be to hole the shot, subject to obstacles and hazards that make taking dead aim at the pin too risky. From a 9-iron to a 4-iron, you should be focusing on a target area that is no more than 2 to 3 yards in circular dimension. For rescue clubs, fairway woods and drivers, you should be choosing a target area that is 3 to 7 yards in circular dimension. You need to maintain a focus on such tight targets to achieve the best shots possible with the understanding that shots that end up within 20 to 35 feet of your target, from a 9-iron to a rescue club, are in some cases better than the PGA Tour Average.

Note: For good ball strikes on full shots, 9-iron through driver, the greatest shot dispersion will typically be to the right or left of the target area rather than longer or shorter. Again, depending on your skill level, from half PW down to chip shots, the greatest shot dispersion will typically be long or short rather than left or right.

The second thing you must do is determine the distance needed for the shot to be played. Once you determine your target, you need to calculate the *gross yardage* of the shot to be played, which is the actual distance between your ball and landing area as well as any estimated roll out. After this, you need to calculate the *net yardage*, or the amount of distance that the ball will carry and roll out to once you factor in all the variables (wind, elevation change, lie, temperature, etc.). This is the step that is most difficult since it takes knowledge, practice and experience to get a mental feel for how the variables affect your shots. Not only do you need the *net yardage* to your target area, but you should also calculate the *net yardage* to safety. This means the minimum distance your ball needs to carry to clear an obstacle or hazard short of your target and the maximum distance your ball can carry and roll out to avoid an obstacle or hazard long of your target. Obstacles and hazards to the right and left must also be considered. For example, a very narrow green is guarded by seven bunkers right and left of the green, and the pin is sitting deep in the green past the bunkers. It may be wise to carry your ball past the bunkers and allow it to roll out to a safe area at the back of the green. It is a must to know how to calculate these distances so you can make a knowledgeable and confident shot decision.

Once you've determined a target and calculated distance(s), you need to analyze all of the variables that could affect your shot. The following is a detailed breakdown. Needless to say, there are other unique variables that may arise during the course of play that we will not address, i.e. mud on your ball, but these are the basics.

Wind

Typically, wind is the most important variable. Earlier you established a general benchmark for the prevailing wind direction and speed and marked that on your scorecard, but now, for individual shots, you need to be more specific. **We believe wind is the most complex variable to evaluate when you're playing.** Its complexity stems from how difficult it is to accurately judge its effects on a shot, and how it may affect your swing and the ball's flight direction and trajectory. The true direction and speed of the wind can constantly change, more so in crosswinds. Therefore, in order to play well in wind, you need substantial practice and experience. Ask yourself, "Has anyone ever explicitly taught me about the wind's effects, and if

Information Gathering (Phase One)

so, how much effort have we spent practicing with that base knowledge?" We believe that most golfers need to spend more time studying and practicing how wind affects their shots.

There are certain fundamentals that we need to know about the wind:

- *The higher you hit the golf ball, the more the wind will affect the flight and thus the distance and direction it will travel.*
- *Crosswinds and gusts make it difficult to consistently predict the wind's effect on the ball. So when this condition exists you must give yourself more room for error.*
- *Wind has a greater effect on the golf ball when the ball is flying into the wind as opposed to flying with the wind.*

There are calculations you can use to estimate how much farther or less far the ball will carry and the direction, but they really are inexact equations because much of the differential is determined by the trajectory and spin of the ball. Trajectory and spin is largely controlled by many variables, such as lie of the ball, grass conditions, and one's swing speed and swing path, making everything that much more complicated.

That being said, the first general rule for wind is as follows:

- *1 mph of headwind adds .8 to .9 % to the gross yardage.*

For example, a 10-mph headwind will cause a 150 yard shot to be played about 8.5%, or 12.75 yards, longer, or 162.75 net yards; typically one club length greater. A 20-mph headwind at 150 yards will create the equivalent of a 176-yard shot to be played.

A tailwind does not affect the ball as much as a headwind. When you have a tailwind the rule of thumb is:

- *1 mph of tailwind lowers the yardage to be played by .4 %.*

So on a 150-yard shot, a 10-mph tailwind will result in a net yardage of 144 yards or 6 yards less. A 20-mph tailwind will shorten a 150-yard shot by 12 yards resulting in the need to strike the ball as if hitting a 138- yard shot.

As for cross winds, the rule is that:

- *The ball gets pushed 1/3 of a yard per mile per hour of wind, per 100 yards.*

For example, if there is a crosswind of 10 mph (+) from the right and the shot is 200 yards, then the ball will be pushed 6 yards to the left (1/3 yard x 10mph = 3 yards x 2 (because the shot is 200 yards) = 6 yards). You would need to aim 6 yards more to the right.

Lastly:

- *Wind can accentuate or dampen the effects of fades and draws.*

If the ball's flight plays against the direction of a crosswind, i.e. a fade into a right to left wind, then the curve of flight will be less pronounced. Conversely, if it flies with the crosswind direction then the curve will be greater. For example, if the wind is coming from the right and you fade the ball into the wind, then the wind will minimize how far the ball fades and also decrease overall distance. The opposite is true if you are playing a draw in right-to-left winds.

The above calculations apply to what the shot does in the air. You need to note that:

- *A tailwind causes a ball to roll out farther than normal, a headwind, less.*

If the wind is coming at an angle, knowledge, feel, and instinct need to take over, and that can only come from experience. Tooled with these general rules of thumb, you should practice with this knowledge, and most importantly, note how the wind affects your ball during rounds. Replay unique shots in your mind and over time, as your library of knowledge grows, you will have a stronger mental feel for how the wind affects your individual shots, thus giving you increased confidence and control in more difficult situations.

Elevation Change

On many courses, your shots will often be either uphill or downhill, which affects the net yardage. Here is the rule of thumb:

- *For every club from driver through 6-iron, add 1 net yard to be played for every 4 feet or 1.33 yards increase in course elevation. Vice versa for downhill shots.*

Let's say the shot is 175 yards, your typical 5-iron, but plays uphill 15 feet (5 yards). That shot will now play as if it was 179 yards (15 feet of elevation divided by 4 feet per yard equals a 3.75 yard increase in yardage to be played.) If the change in elevation were 30 feet, that 175-yard shot would become a 183-yard shot.

- *From 7-iron down to PW: add approximately 1 net yard for every 3 feet or 1 yard of elevation change. Vice versa for downhill shots.*

Example: A 125 yard 9-iron shot with a target 20 feet below you will play as if it was a 118 yards.

Note: The flatter your standard ball flight, the more you need to adjust for elevation change; the higher you hit your shots, the less you have to adjust.

Since devices that measure elevation change are not allowed by the rules put in place by the USGA and R&A, you'll need to use *mental calculations and feel to* gauge elevation change. This can be tough since quite often there are optical illusions on the golf course, such as false fronts near the green. Additionally, gradual inclines and declines over the length of a hole can be difficult to see and therefore calculate, though they pack a heavy punch on the net yardage. Mental imaging can be a good tool to use here. For example, try to picture your 6-foot tall friend standing at your target area and use this as a base to judge the elevation change. Once again, this all comes down to your knowledge and experience from playing a previous hole or similar holes in the past and noting the affect on the shot. This, coupled with the knowledge of the approximate formula guidelines, will give you the best chance for success.

Note: One can use a range finder that measures elevation change in practice rounds to help you check your calculations and feel against the range finder.

Ball Position Relative to Stance

This is the most personal of all the elements considered in the Information Gathering Phase because the result from a given lie varies significantly with your swing (flat, upright, etc.) and with your standard ball flight (fade, draw, low trajectory, high trajectory). The best way to learn to adjust for different kinds of lies, uphill, downhill, sidehill, fairway, rough, etc. is to practice shots under all of these conditions and build your library of knowledge.

Begin with the basic knowledge that (for right-handed players):

- *Most shots hit with the ball above your feet will curve left*
- *Most shots with the ball below your feet will curve right*
- *Shots hit from an uphill lie will tend to fly higher and left*
- *Those from a downhill lie will tend to fly lower and right*

Through practice and play, work out the extent to which those tendencies apply to your shots by using some simple rules of thumb as a base:

- *For every one-inch above or below your feet, adjust about 5 yards for shots hit with a 6- to 9-iron.*
- *Adjust about 7 to 8 yards for those hit with a 5-iron to driver.*

Again, these are adjustments you need to work out for yourself through practice and play. Don't just wing it; do the homework to make a good choice when it comes to lie of the ball.

Grass Conditions of Rough, Fairways and Greens

If your round is set to start early in the morning, when it is typically cooler outside, dew could still be present. This can slow the fairway and greens, thus allowing for less rollout. Throughout your round though, the temperature may rise quickly, drying out the grass and greens, making conditions more firm and fast.

If the fairways are firm, you will get more roll than in soft conditions. That will create more math to figure when planning your shot because you must take into account the run out, or lack thereof. You should also get a sense of what the turf is like in front of the greens. If it's firm, you will want to play for shorter carry on your approach shots to allow for the bounce you will get in front of the green. If it's soft, then you will know that you must carry approach shots onto the green to avoid leaving shots short of your target on the green.

If it's wet in the rough, it's tougher to get the club head through the ball, which costs you distance, as opposed to dry conditions when the club can pass through more easily. In some cases, you might even hit the ball further than you would off the fairway because the ball is sitting comfortably on a "bird's nest stuffed with feathers." That's called a "flyer lie." And obviously, the density of the grass, regardless of whether it's wet or dry, will alter how you hit the ball. Even to the extent that if the rough is too long and thick, the only play you might have is to hack the ball to the fairway and take your medicine, U.S. Open style. You should also keep in mind that grass conditions typically change throughout the year with the seasons. In spring for example, due to the rain and cooler temperatures, the ball will not travel as far, whereas in the middle of summer the course tends to dry out a bit giving more roll and bounce to your shots. In some southern states, i.e. Florida, the grass may thicken from June to October, so this is also location dependent.

A lot of the initial feel and planning for the grass conditions can be completed before you tee off. The pre-round analysis will make your decisions easier and quicker to evaluate during the round.

Information Gathering (Phase One)

Flight Path & Visualization

Now that you've determined a target, calculated your distance and analyzed all the necessary variables, you need to determine and visualize the ball's flight path. We further expand upon this concept of flight path visualization in the next chapter, but we need to introduce the basic principle now since it is such a critical component for one's shot determination.

Visualization is the process by which you use mental imagery to see your ball travel down a start line and subsequently see the ball curve toward its target. Even for very good golfers, shots do not fly perfectly straight. The ball will either draw or fade off your start line, even if only slightly. Thus one's start line is always to the right or left of one's target. The best way to visualize is to pick a distant object on your start line, see your ball flying towards this distant object, then curving off the start line and ending up at its target.

At this point in Information Gathering, you've nailed down a target and distance, you've taken into account the wind, your elevation, lie of the ball, etc., you should have a strong mental feel for the shot, and you've begun to visualize the ensuing shot in your mind. Once you pull a club from your bag and begin to lightly grip and re-grip, you begin to transfer the mental image and feel for the shot into a physical feel, through your fingers, hands and arms. Most importantly, you're absolutely positive (if not, start again) about the information that you've gathered. Thus, you are confident. You can commit to the shot to be played.

Information Gathering has ended.

EXAMPLE SCENARIO

Consider the following scenario set at Augusta National, one of the world's greatest courses. There are many factors and variables that can affect each shot and complexity levels vary. You can use this example scenario as a general shot process guideline and supplement it with the relevant variables. The example will give you a good idea of how to use the Information Gathering Phase within the shot process.

It's the par-3 12th hole at Augusta National, at Amen Corner, where so much drama has occurred on the final day of many Masters Tournaments; as we saw in the Jordan Spieth narrative earlier. The 12th hole is a devilish hole that demands perfection in one's information-gathering abilities. At No. 12 the wind can swirl in different directions throughout the day. Therefore it can be tough to gauge exactly how it's going to be

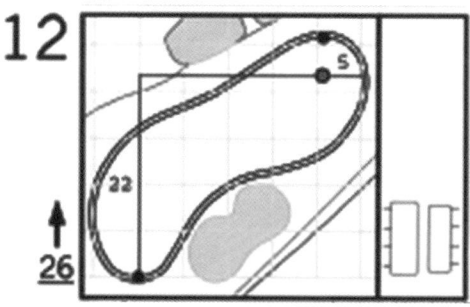

blowing from one minute to the next. Rae's Creek is looming in front of the green and there is a pair of bunkers guarding much of the back of the green. There's also a bunker in front and a very shallow green depth of 11 to 16 yards depending on any particular cross section. On this difficult hole, determining the target (area), correct gross and net yardages, and the flight path, is as important as the shot execution itself.

In this scenario, the pin placement is typical of that on the final day of a Masters Tournament. The pin is to the back right on the diagonal green, just 5 yards from the right edge and 5 from the back edge. The temperature is 80 degrees and the wind is forecast to be from 7 to 10 miles per hour from the right and towards the tees at about a 45-degree angle. In this scenario, picture that you are a right handed player with a 2 handicap that typically fades the ball.

The first step in the Information Gathering Phase is to choose a target area (a 2 to 3 yard circle for iron shots of this length). Given the fact that you are fortunate enough to be playing at the beautiful and legendary Augusta National and that you've been swinging confidently and free, you decide not to play to safety and aim for a shorter shot to the deeper left side of the green. Instead, you decide to take a more direct line to the pin that places the hole directly in the middle of your 2-3 yard target circle. You are quickly reminded however, that the wind (which is the most significant factor on this shot, as with most other full-swing shots in golf) is angling from the right, slightly into your face. Recognizing the hazards and trouble areas, you know it's better to miss long and left here, taking the creek out of play, which runs in front of the green angling away from the tee slightly. There isn't much green behind the pin or to the right of it, but it's better to be through the green in the second cut or even in a bunker than in the water. So you adjust your target area accordingly, about 2 to 3 yards left and a yard behind the pin. After all, you tend to fade the ball, which will fight against the mild breeze angling from the right and should cancel out the fade nicely, producing a nearly straight flight path. Now that you have determined your target area, you can look through that spot to find a distant object in line with your target. Noticing that there is a red colored azalea that stands out about 15 yards behind and in line with your target area, that's the distant object you choose as your start line. Normally, your start line would be further left, but do to the right to left wind, the start line is straighter to your target for this shot. The **gross yardage** to your target area is 158 yards and, following this line, it will take a 150-yard shot to carry the steep bank at the front of the green and the slope that runs to Rae's Creek.

Now you need to figure out the **net yardage.** The wind is always a difficult factor on this hole, coming from the right and in your face at a 45-degree angle at approximately 7-10 miles per hour. Based on the experience that you've gained by playing in this type of wind, you decide that the wind will add about 6-8 yards to the distance you need to play. Since your shot type is a fade, the ball will fly at an increased angle approaching perpendicular to the wind lessening its affects plus, as you noted earlier, it's better to be long on this shot. As such, you decide to play the shot 8 yards longer. Due to the higher temperature today, you've also noticed that your ball has been carrying an extra 2 yards all day long, bringing the added yardage down to 6 yards. There is a slight drop in elevation from tee to green but its effects are basically negligible. All relevant factors considered now, the net yardage to your landing area is 164 yards, but just 156 yards to safely clear the creek, bank, and front bunker.

You know that your stock 7-iron will carry 155 yards, which isn't adequate. However, if you hit it strong, you could get 160 out of it leaving you on the green a few yards short of the pin. You know this could mess with your tempo, though, and even the slightest mishit here could leave your ball in significant trouble. The other option is to hit your stock 6-iron, which goes 165 yards. Once again, you recognize it is safer to miss a bit long, and if you hit a slightly softer 6-iron, you should be right where you want without any added mechanical swing thoughts. Lastly, knowing that a slightly stronger fade is required to flight the ball into the right to left wind; your "feel swing thought" is to hold off a bit to produce a more pronounced fade to ensure the ball works into the wind.

Confident in your analysis, you now have club in hand and your target and net yardages settled. With both shot visualization and mental feel in your mind, you are ready to move into the Pre-Swing Phase with a confident and committed decision. Execute the swing and shot you planned and you will have a good opportunity to secure a birdie on one of the most renowned par-3's in the world.

Once you gain experience with this method, this calculation should take place in about a minute or so. (Note this is a complex analysis and most shots shouldn't take this long, especially with stock shots and courses that you are familiar with.) Once you've made your decision about conditions and club selection, there's no second-guessing, no turning back, unless conditions or variables change.

This scenario takes much longer to read (on paper) than to experience when you're on a course. As we've said, in contrast to the next two phases, the time you spend in the **Information Gathering** phase can vary considerably from shot to shot in this phase. But some of this deliberation and calculation can be done as you're on your way to the next tee or your ball, especially if you're playing a course you know well.

Once you've considered all the factors affecting your shot, and you've decided on a club, you should have a strong mental feel for how you want the shot to fly, where it will land, and where it should stop. Then you see your start line and the ball curving and ending at the target (visualization). At this point, review your decision and take yourself through the anticipated shot one last time. The following is what thoughts can go on in your mind once you've worked your way through the shot analysis during the Information Gathering phase:

"This is a soft stock 6-iron for me. My start line is the light-pink azalea I chose as my distant object behind the green. I see little to no curve in the ball's flight to the target, for the right to left wind will work against my fade. The ball will land just over the right side of the bunker in the front to middle portion of the green and roll about 10 feet toward the back-right pin. I'll hit my soft stock 6-iron, just as I did three holes before, holding off the release just a bit longer to make sure I get a good left-to-right flight path. I'm instinctively confident I've made the right decision and have the right club. No doubts. I'm confident, committed and ready to go."

As Jack Nicklaus wrote in his classic book, *Golf My Way,* "I feel that hitting specific shots- playing the ball to a certain place in a certain way is 50 percent mental picture, 40 percent setup and 10 percent swing."

Or put another way, as said by 5-time British Open champion Peter Thompson, *"The most important facets of golf are careful planning, calm and clear thinking, and the ordinary logic of common sense."* That kind of planning helps to eliminate second-guessing and doubt about the club or kind of shot you intend to hit.

Note: All Tour Pros and their caddies use a yardage book to help them determine many of the issues that have been discussed in this chapter. Their yardage books and personal notes remind them, among other things, where the greens slope as well as the potential trouble spots around the greens. Many players keep and update their books so that they can use the knowledge and experience they've compiled from previous years in the years to come.

Before Payne Stewart played in and won the 1999 US Open at Pinehurst, he and his instructor Chuck Cook devised a strategy to shade in, with a red marker, all the areas in his yardage book where missing a shot would create difficulty or spell disaster around the greens. It is believed that this method, used in his information gathering routine, was instrumental in his win.

SUMMARY POINTS

- Information Gathering phase consists of: determining a target (area), calculating the gross and net yardages for the shot to be played after analyzing the variables that could affect the shot (wind, elevation change, lie, etc.), choosing a flight path, starting the visualization, and acquiring your mental feel and initial physical feel for the shot. The exact order of shot determination can vary from shot to shot and player to player. At this point, you must be confident in your decision and thus can commit to your shot.
- The Information Gathering phase has a definitive end. If you are not confident and committed at the end of this phase, you need to stop and re-evaluate the shot, i.e. your target area, the variables, visualization and mental feel, until you are confident. Identify and correct any weak link(s) until you are confident. You can only move on to the Pre-Swing Phase when you are 100% confident in your decision so that you can commit.

- There isn't a time limit in this phase but you should be considerate of your fellow golfers. Most importantly, you want to stay ready to perform athletically without bogging yourself down. As you learn to instinctively gather and consolidate all the information in this phase, it will become easier and quicker for you over time.
- The greatest challenge in mastering Information Gathering phase extends beyond the mathematical calculations of all the information. There's no possible way to teach you how to analyze every condition you'll encounter on the course and their combined effect. Information Gathering will only become second nature through knowledge, practice and experience, and in becoming so, will give you the ability to shoot lower scores and a substantial edge over your fellow golfers.

See video for this chapter at:
http://golfs8secondsecret.com/book-chapter-videos/

4

THE PRE-SWING
(PHASE TWO)

"Hesitation is a very bad thing in golf. Let the player think as much as he likes before he comes to a conclusion as to what he is going to try to do, and what club he is going to take for the purpose; but, having taken his club, it will be far better for the prospects of his shot if he dismisses the question of any alternatives absolutely from his mind."

-Advanced Golf, *by James Braid, a 5-time British Open champion-*

THE PRE-SWING PHASE is the second phase of the shot process. The Pre-Swing phase and the final phase, the Swing phase, are controlled by four key elements: the amount of time spent in the phase, athletic and sufficient movements, having a clear visualization and strong physical feel. In the Pre-Swing phase, we will predominantly focus on one's visualization and physical feel, which are the two critical elements of this phase. We will also discuss both the timing and movements that are key elements in this phase.

The first objective of your Pre-Swing is to "see" a clear mental picture of your flight path (visualization) for the shot. The second is to merge one's visualization and mental feel to obtain the physical feel (which includes your mechanical swing thoughts, i.e., a complete shoulder turn, turn my hips on down swing, etc.) through a practice swing(s). *Note: when we say to "obtain physical feel," it means that you're bringing the initial physical feel you have acquired to this point in the shot process and strengthening it by adding your visualization and mental feel through to the practice swing. Furthermore, you will likely strengthen your physical feel even more through your waggle(s) in the Swing phase (more on this in the next chapter).* Both of these elements will allow you to narrow your focus and for your swing to begin to take on a more subconscious behavior. In essence, this phase is a bridge between the conscious considerations of the Information Gathering Phase and the largely subconscious and instinctive movements of the Swing phase.

As we've said earlier, it's the blurring of the Information Gathering, Pre-Swing & Swing phases that bring so many golfers to question their decisions, thus limiting their confidence and commitment and allowing for doubt and distraction. Remember, you're no longer gathering information here; you have all the information you need. You're no longer debating your target, which club you should hit, or the flight path. You've already made those decisions. Your goal is to rehearse the swing, confirm your visualization and obtain and confirm your physical feel. Here, your focus will naturally begin to narrow in preparation for the final swing itself as you concentrate solely on these two elements.

By allowing only a certain amount of time for these actions to take place there will be little to no room for you to think about anything else. Your overall movements should also begin to energize your body and keep tension at bay. At the end of this phase you should still be confident, committed (even more so than after the Information

Gathering phase), and zeroed in on your visualization with a strong physical feel for the swing phase.

TIME LIMITATION

After reviewing footage of the great players, we found that they limited the amount of time they took in the pre-swing phase. However, more so in the Pre-Swing phase than in The Swing phase, there was some variance in their timing, depending on how they personally executed the steps in the phase. The average amount of time they spent was about 12 seconds, plus or minus. Prior to the Faldo Era, the amount of time was a little quicker at 6 to 10 seconds, while after the Faldo Era, the time spent in this phase has been 12 seconds (+ or -). Also, this time can vary depending on the number of practice swing(s) you take and the degree to which you visualize the flight path of the ball, which we will explain later in the chapter. Regardless, you should not deviate longer than the 12 second recommendation. The 12-second time limitation encourages your mind to focus solely on the visualization and physical feel elements involved during this phase. Twelve seconds should be all you need; much more time and you might let in unnecessary conscious thoughts and/or perform unnecessary actions. If one is to error, it should be on being quicker than 12 seconds.

Note: We believe that the amount of time players spend in their routines has increased for a couple of reasons. One reason for this, as we discussed earlier, is because feel has decreased in recent decades. Therefore, it takes longer for players to obtain feel for any one shot. Secondly, there has been a stronger emphasis on visualization by both instructors and golf psychologists more recently, which takes more time. We believe that both actions help you swing more instinctively, but have led to longer pre-swing phases.

So What Happens In Those 12 Seconds?

The Pre-Swing Phase is a dress rehearsal for your final swing. You need to perform the following in this phase: a trigger, shot visualization, followed by merging the visualization and mental feel to obtain your physical feel (which includes your mechanical swing thoughts) through practice swing(s). The exact order and to what degree can vary, but you must be consistent with the routine you develop from shot to shot. For example, Phil Mickelson appears to do visualization first, then two practice swings, and then visualize again a few seconds before moving into the swing phase. Tom Watson on the other hand appears to take a longer look (visualization or some form of it) before his practice swing and then goes directly into the swing phase, looking at the target as he actively places his right foot to start the swing phase. What's important is that you incorporate these actions (trigger, visualization, merge visualization and mental feel to obtain physical feel through a practice swing) into your own pre-swing routine and complete them in 12 seconds or less.

MOVEMENT

It's important to stay physically active in this phase, for the "dance" has begun. As you visualize your shot and develop your physical feel, the movements might be as small as slight, relaxing grip adjustments or a shift in one's feet. Outside of the shot visualization part of this phase, your body should be engaged in movement that will help you start to energize and help with the physical feel. Put another way, you should have consistent and sufficient enough movement to carry an athletic feel into the Swing phase. If you look at the greats, most, if not all, had an aura of vitality and energy. Think back on Trevino, Ballesteros, and Tiger Woods for example. They may have paused slightly to focus on their mental picture at certain points, depending on their own unique routines, but they consistently had movements to help them stay athletic and maintain and/or build up positive energy.

SHOT VISUALIZATION

"Mental rehearsal is just as important as physical rehearsal."
-Phil Mickelson-

Visualization is taking your intended ball's flight path for the shot to be played, and converting it into a "movie" (the ball's flight). This allows you to clearly "see" and define the shot to be executed.

Visualization is a strong tool because our subconscious has a difficult time distinguishing between vivid mental pictures and "real-life" experiences. When you perform shot visualization, it can almost be as if you've already performed the shot. If you can picture yourself hitting the shot that you want, then your brain can begin to program your muscles to feel and replicate the results. With this tool, your brain has an easier and better chance to repeat this in the actual swing.

There are two different methods of shot visualization that we subscribe to. The first is what we call, "Complete Visualization", and the second is called "Intermediate Target Visualization". We recommend and use the Complete Visualization method.

Complete Visualization

Visualization is the process by which you use mental imagery to see your ball travel along a start line and subsequently see the ball curve off the start line towards its target. The ball will either draw or fade off your start line, even if only slightly. Thus your start line is always to the right or left of your target. The best way to visualize is to pick a distant object on your start line and see your ball curving off the start line and ending up at your target. For example, let's say you're a golfer that has a slight fade, up to 5 yards, and you're 175 yards out from a center-placed pin. If you take dead aim at the pin your ball will end up on the right side or edge of the green. Instead you adjust your *starting line* to a point at the *left edge* of the green using a tree trunk behind the green about 3 yards to the right of the greenside bunker on the left, so that your fade has room to work and move towards your target (the pin).

Essentially, you can break down your visualization into three parts: 1) its initial launch down the starting line towards a distant object, 2) its curved release (draw or fade) off the starting line towards your target (area), and 3) the ball stopping at your target (area).

Intermediate Target Visualization

Jack Nicklaus popularized the intermediate target method and it is now an accepted teaching method, and also the practice of many golf pros and accomplished amateurs.

To use this method, one uses the complete visualization method with the addition of an intermediate target which is a spot typically 1 to 3 feet in front of the ball. The spot may be an old divot, a discolored bit of grass, a twig or anything that you can use as a focusing point. This intermediate point can help with alignment and will remind you again where the initial ball direction needs to start. You should have a mental image of your ball flying over this spot down the starting line, and then curving toward your end target (area).

We don't recommend this method for these four reasons: 1) we've noticed overwhelmingly that players using this method tend to line up to the right of the starting line. This is because the golfer is standing beside the ball and looking at an angle to their intermediate target. It's like holding a gun out to your side and trying to hit a target down range. That's difficult to do accurately. 2) Most golfers don't choose a starting line that allows for sufficient curve (draw or fade) that takes place. They tend to choose an intermediate target that is straighter to their target area. This of course means that their ball would have to fly relatively straight in order to end up at their target. We know that nearly all shots curve, so their ball would be moving away from the target accordingly.

3) Golfers typically don't paint as complete a flight path or produce a "movie" for the shot to be played as they would using a complete visualization method. 4) If your intermediate target is off by a few inches, then after traveling 175 yards that inch mistake may turn into a miscalculation of approximately 5 yards (plus).

Don't get us wrong, if you have experienced success using this method and are comfortable with it, then don't fix something that's not broken. However, you can and should test yourself against the four issues above to see if you can bring about improvement.

Two Notes On Visualization

You need to realize that few, if any, of your shots will fly perfectly straight. As we mentioned earlier, almost all shots either draw or fade, and this holds true even for the best golfers.

If you have trouble picturing the "movie" it may help to ask yourself what you want to happen. For example: "I see my ball flying down the start line towards my distant object which is the trunk of the oak tree behind the left side of the green. Then the ball will fade 3 yards towards my target (area). The ball ends up at my target which is 1 yard to the left of the pin."

Some golfers prefer more elaborate visualizations where they picture how high the ball will fly, etc. However, we find that detail unnecessary for stock shots because it adds to more time being spent in the phase.

FEEL

Mental and physical feel is of great importance in The Pre-Swing phase; and this has always been the case whether one was swinging hickory, steel, or graphite. Percy Boomer, one of golf's most influential early teachers insisted on his pupils learning golf through muscle memory. He asserted that *the feel of correct mechanics* led to the best golf.

In his book, *On Learning Golf*, Boomer wrote:

> "*The difference between the good and the ordinary golfer is that the good one feels his shot through address. Whether or not he has learned deliberately to play by feel, the good player feels, through his carriage and balance... [in] the coming movements that will bring his clubface squarely against the ball.*"

Recall that earlier in this book we defined two separate types of feel, mental and physical. Though we have defined them, they are still quite difficult to teach due to their nature. However, following the basic fundamentals of the pre-swing phase will allow you to strengthen your physical feel over time. Physical feel comes from the fundamental feel of your swing, i.e. proper grip, posture, stance, swing plane, etc., all the way through to the balanced finish. Over time you can call on that vault of good swings and shots that you've practiced and experienced and incorporate the mental feel you gained from those shots into your practice swing (in the Pre-Swing phase) and Swing phase. Again, one of the goals of the practice swing is to merge visualization and mental feel to obtain your physical feel. Again, feel, at the most basic level, is the mind and the body working as one.

MECHANICAL SWING THOUGHT(S)

We have never read or heard anything about the greatest players not having at least one (1) or more mechanical swing thoughts during their shot process. Mechanical swing thoughts are conscious to semi-conscious thoughts to perform or impart a certain physical action during one's swing, i.e. maintain one's spine angle or keep one's head steady, etc. There is a big difference between trying to bring about a substantial change to one's swing through rigorous and thought driven practice sessions on the range or course which involve very "hard" conscious thought(s), versus the "soft" or fleeting conscious thoughts that arise when one has achieved swing change(s) and has been swinging reasonably well.

Again, mechanical swing thoughts should be intertwined with one's physical feel for the swing to be executed in the Pre-Swing phase.

The reason for this is two-fold. The first is that you only have two critical elements during the swing phase: visualization and physical feel, and the way to optimize your physical feel is to integrate it with your mechanical swing thought(s). Let's go back to the earlier scenario at the 12th hole of Augusta. The player is going to hold off his shot a little. This is part of his physical feel. What mechanical swing thought(s) a player uses to do this can vary, i.e. maybe they delay their release a little or make more of a cut swing through the ball, etc. Again, because this player is swinging well to this point in the round, and for the most part this is a stock shot for this player, his conscious mechanical swing thoughts should be fleeting. Secondly, we want one's focus to be as narrow and subconscious as possible. This is achieved by solely limiting your thoughts to visualization and physical feel, which in turn helps you limit distractions and stay in the present.

Remember, when swinging reasonably well you're trying to swing as subconsciously and instinctively as possible. When you do, you will play your best golf. *Again, the "hard" conscious mechanical swing thoughts one makes between pure practice and the "soft" conscious fleeting swing thoughts that occur when playing well are different. When fleeting mechanical swing thoughts are achieved, they are one of the catalysts for freer swings when you're playing well and trying to finish off a good round.*

In the Pre-Swing phase, visualization and mental feel are merged. This will solidify the shot and swing to be executed by syncing your brain and your body.

THE TRIGGER

A trigger action signals the start of your pre-swing phase. It reaffirms that the considerations from Information-Gathering should no longer be consciously thought about, unless conditions change. From here on out, you should be intently focused on the task at hand, rehearsing the shot and swing to be played. Examples of possible triggers could be closing the Velcro on your glove, touching your cap, taking your place behind the ball and focusing in on the target, or setting your club in one hand or the other at your side. Whatever you choose, make sure your trigger is simple and repeatable.

PRACTICE SWING

As mentioned before, the objectives of the practice swing(s) are to: merge your visualization and mental feel to obtain your physical feel (which includes one or two mechanical swing thought(s)) while

The Pre-Swing (Phase Two)

rehearsing the shot and swing to be executed. A few of the greats took more than one practice swing, but the majority of them appear to only take one. We recommend one practice swing for most shots because the majority of your golf shots will be stock swings/shots, and therefore you should be able to merge your visualization and mental feel to obtain your physical feel without too much effort. For unique or situational shots, two or even three swings is normal and recommended. It is a personal choice whether you take one or two practice swings for stock swings/shots.

Three key points of the practice swing are as follows:

1) First, you should aim for a club head speed of about 70 to 90% of the swing you plan to execute.

   *Note: Most of the greats we've studied do not make half-hearted motions or half-swings, which leads us to the second key point.

2) You should substantially complete the backswing and most importantly, the follow through. Don't stop your swing at impact or perform a half-pass. Complete the swing. Remember, it's a swing, not a hit. Also, the "wave" or partial swing that some golfers make during their routines short circuits the process and introduces a motion different than the one you really want to execute and can confuse your body. Again, you are trying to create a baseline for the Swing Phase so your body knows how to perform when it comes time to execute.

3) You should brush the ground with your practice swing(s). Swinging above the ground is a bit of a false rehearsal with the exception of a practice swing(s) with your driver off a tee.

For shots from a PW down to chips, we advise that you rehearse your practice swing(s) while standing alongside the ball instead of behind it. As previously mentioned, your greatest shot dispersion tends to be either long or short of your target from shots at this range. Therefore, standing alongside your ball gives you the best feel possible for the distance. we also recommend 2 or 3 practice swings for these shots because these typically aren't stock shots, and by default, are unique.

PUTTING THE PIECES TOGETHER

Now that we have gone through the individual components that go into The Pre-Swing Phase, let's go through it step by step.

While standing about 2 to 4 paces behind the ball, perpendicular to and looking towards the target (area), initiate your trigger. This signals for you to begin an initial visualization (2 to 4 seconds) for the shot, during which you pick a distant object on your start line and see your ball curving off the start line and ending up at your target (area). Next, turn your body so that you are parallel to your start line, setting your feet into an approximately normal stance. Complete a practice swing at a speed of around 70 to 90% of the swing you plan to execute. The goal of the practice swing is to provide the bridge to merge one's visualization and mental feel to obtain your physical feel (including mechanical swing thoughts). Once you've completed your practice swing(s), turn perpendicular to and face your start line once more. It is here that you will complete your final visualization (we believe it should be a little shorter (more fleeting) than the initial visualization (2 to 3 seconds)). All the while you should grip and re-grip the club, and possibly perform a slight waggle of the club to continue to build on the physical feel which should be traveling up through your arms and shoulders, along with slight movement in your feet to maintain energy for the shot and swing that you've dress-rehearsed. You then turn 45° to 75° to your start line, take a step to the left, then take 2 or 4 steps to move into the swing phase, thus ending the Pre-Swing Phase and beginning the Swing Phase. You have a 12 second time limit from the time you initiate your trigger to move into the Swing Phase, all the while remaining in sufficient and athletic motion.

If at any time you are uncomfortable in the Pre-Swing Phase, or do not feel 100% confident or committed to executing the Swing Phase as you have planned, then it is here that you must stop to re-group. Perhaps you need to go back to the Information-Gathering Phase (if it's information related) or re-start the Pre-Swing Phase if it concerns visualization and feel. Think about it… If you don't "feel right" at the end of this phase, you're not going to be confident and committed to your final swing.

MAINTAINING A ROUTINE

Consistency is one of the keys that allow the components of the Pre-Swing Phase to work so well. If your routine is inconsistent in your visualization, actions in obtaining your physical feel, the movements you make, or the time spent in the phase, it will not hold strong, thus producing inconsistent results. One of the main strengths of this phase, and the Swing Phase, is that they will set you up, time and time again in the same way (and eventually, it will become instinctive) to hit more of your best golf shots. If the moments leading into the swing phase vary from shot to shot, then this phase will not deliver the maximum results it was designed to deliver. Likewise, if your body receives different commands each time you go into the swing phase, then the muscle memory, and thus the feel that Percy Boomer stresses, will not have the best chance to become a strong tool.

SUMMARY POINTS

- The elements in the **Pre-Swing** phase are:
  1) Shot visualization 2) obtaining and maintaining physical feel 3) the amount of time spent in the phase, and 4) athletic and sufficient movement. Visualization and physical feel are the critical elements in this phase.
- The Trigger signals to your brain that your Pre-Swing phase has started and it is time to focus tightly on the task at hand. The Pre-Swing phase ends as you place your lead foot to begin to establish your stance in the Swing phase.
- A practice swing is needed because it merges one's visualization and mental feel with the physical feel (which includes your mechanical swing thoughts).
- The Pre-Swing phase should take you 12 seconds or less.
- Your movements should be consistent and sufficient to relieve muscle tension and start to build energy for the Swing Phase.
- You should have carried over the confidence you gathered during Information Gathering into this phase. If your confidence decreases at any point during the Pre-Swing phase, you need to stop and start over. Re-evaluate whether the information you gathered doesn't feel correct, in which case you need to go back to the Information Gathering phase, or if you don't have a clear visualization or physical feel for the shot to be played, you need to start the Pre-Swing phase over.
- Your routine is simple and easily repeatable so you are consistent time and time again.

See video for this chapter at:
http://golfs8secondsecret.com/book-chapter-videos/

5

THE SWING
(PHASE THREE)

"The golf swing happens far too fast for you consciously to direct your muscles. Frequently we can make very minor adjustments in midswing, but they are always instinctive, never conscious."
-Golf My Way, *by Jack Nicklaus*-

This is it, the third and final phase in the shot process. Of all of the phases, this one is the most critical because it is where everything comes together and the shot is executed. *It is mostly in the swing phase where it appears the greatest major champions are most similar with the elements and have separated themselves from their fellow competitors.* These players seem to have a common trait beyond their otherworldly talents, and it's this: They have perfected a simple, time limited and movement filled, repetitive swing phase that promotes powerful, free and instinctive swings that stand up to the pressures they face in the most critical of moments, most notably when coming down the stretch in the biggest tournaments. Essentially, this seems to allow them to consistently hit high quality stock and unique shots. Think of Phil Mickelson's iconic second shot from behind the trees and off the pine needles on the 13th hole during the final round of the 2010 Masters.

In this chapter we will go through the instruction, step-by-step, of the time limitation, movements to be made, visualization and physical feel. *This phase places the greatest emphasis on the time limitation and movement elements. Most golfers fail to properly incorporate these elements into their swing phase. Coupled with a strong visualization and physical feel that is brought over from the Pre-Swing phase.* We will show you how to construct a swing phase that will allow you to perform freer swings consistently no matter the pressure threshold.

IT'S A MATTER OF TIME!

One of the four key elements in this book is the importance of being timely, and in this phase, time is one of the two critical elements (possibly the most critical), and hence the basis for the book's title. Time is a factor that has been overlooked for years and its importance has been rarely discussed. You know that you should have a certain tempo or rhythm to your swing, so as not to rush it (more on this later), but we believe it's unlikely that you've read or been taught to hit the ball in a *specific* amount of time. Based upon research and swing analysis of the greats, we found that they progressed through their swing phase in approximately **8 seconds or less,** based on our definitions. Whether it was a conscious limitation or the subconscious result of trial and error over the years (how we believe it came about), it's the byproduct of a non-hesitant swing phase. The time limitation helps to narrowly focus the mind, relieve tension and maintain or increase one's overall energy, all of which helps create a more subconscious swing. Many instructors tell you "don't over think it", to "stay in the present", or the importance of decreasing mental distractions when you swing, but the means to get there have largely been unclear.

The Swing (Phase Three)

The idea behind this strict time limitation (and it is strictly 8 seconds or less) is that your mind and your muscles simply do not have the time to wander or be distracted into negative thinking, and must act primarily subconsciously. At no point during this phase will you debate your club selection or review a checklist of what to do's. The time limitation is the final casing that helps bring everything together and helps you move efficiently through visualization, to physical feel, and into action, leaving little to no room for distraction, doubt and conscious thought. You are in a world of your own where nothing other than visualization and physical feel fills your brain, allowing you to swing instinctively.

Our definition of the swing is different from traditional teachings for it begins earlier, combining much of the "traditional pre-shot routine" and the "traditional swing" in order to eliminate the "break" between the "steps" of the traditional shot process. As we define it, *the Swing Phase begins once your right foot (for right-handed players) is being actively moved into place to establish your stance. This is where the stopwatch begins and you have 8 seconds to complete the swing.* This is important: You **do not** have 8 seconds to start the backswing, but instead, you have 8 seconds to progress through the entire swing phase including the follow through. We're sure some of you may be thinking that this seems a bit fast, and at first, it may seem fast to many, but any longer and you allow time for mental distractions to creep in, muscle tension to increase and energy to decrease, and allow conscious thoughts to direct the show. If you find that your mind is still interfering in this phase, then that is a telltale sign that: 1) you may be uncommitted to the Information Gathering 2) your visualization and/or physical feel might not be clear or strong enough or 3) you are taking too much time in the phase and allowing unnecessary thoughts and tension.

Additionally, the 8 seconds also encourages a narrow focused mind and will help you to "stay in the present," as many teachers call it. Staying in the present, or in the now, is critical during pressure-filled rounds since you are more focused on the task at hand instead of previous, negative, or future outcomes or concerns.

Here the point should be made that we are *not* telling you to rush the swing phase. By no means should you be speeding up your movements, backswing or follow through, otherwise your tempo and rhythm would be compromised. It may take effort and diligent practice for some to learn how to properly limit this phase and establish a comfortable and rhythmic cadence. Some golfers to watch for what is meant by rhythm and cadence are: Ben Hogan, Lee Trevino, Tom Watson and Phil Mickelson. (Their swing phases are on our website.) All four were rhythmical in their routines and performed them in 8 seconds or less. It may be a few months before you experience the full benefits of the 8-second limit, but we assure you that the sooner you adhere to it, the faster this will become second nature and you will experience freer and more instinctive swings.

NICKLAUS

Regarding the time limitation in the Swing Phase, Jack Nicklaus is the one substantial exception of the greats listed on page 23. He typically took 12 to 15 seconds in the swing phase while averaging only 4 to 6 seconds in the Pre-Swing Phase, thus the total amount of time he spent in both phases was 18 to 20 seconds (+ or -). As you know, 20 seconds is our recommended time frame for the combination of the two phases. He appears to do a substantial portion of the Pre-Swing elements in the Swing phase. We believe this is confirmed by a quote from his book, *Golf My Way,* where he states, *"The time to focus your mind on key swing thoughts is as you settle into your final address position."*

Based on this statement and other information in his book, we believe that he is referring to getting one's visualization and physical feel completed, while in address, before starting the backswing. As we've stated, obtaining and confirming one's mental picture (visualization) and physical feel including mechanical swing thought(s) for the shot needs to be completed in the Pre-Swing phase. We believe that most of the greats substantially completed those elements in the Pre-Swing, and thus, their Pre-Swings were longer and Swing Phases shorter than Nicklaus's.

Nicklaus only appears to deviate from the four key elements of the Swing Phase with respect to time. Of the other three elements, he is spot on. He exhibits continuous and rhythmic movement. We also know from his book, *Golf My Way*, that Nicklaus clearly visualizes ("sees the movie") and develops some feel for the shot to be played in the Swing Phase.

MOVEMENT, MOVEMENT, MOVEMENT!

The second most critical element in this phase is movement. In the Swing Phase you should be in continuous and rhythmic motion, which needs to be repetitive and consistent in cadence from swing to swing. The initial movement is started by the placement of the right foot (lead foot) to begin to establish the stance, and continues on with movement in both feet which is carried into the legs and buttocks. It's simultaneously joined by the waggle, bringing movement into the hands and arms. The energy generated from the movements needs to transfer to the backswing with no break. For a brief moment, think back to Chapter One and the narrative about Lee Westwood's final round at Muirfield. One of the weakest elements in Lee Westwood's shot process was the 3-second motionless pause he took before starting his backswing. When you're in the swing phase and your feet are set, if you're standing there largely or completely motionless, then your muscles will tense up and unnecessary thoughts can creep in and zap you of the energy needed for a smooth and strong, primarily subconscious swing. Additionally, this lack of movement will reintroduce some form of the "break" that our shot process and Swing phase is specifically designed to eliminate.

The movements of the feet and legs primarily provide energy and relieve tension in the swing, while the waggle mostly provides physical feel for the swing and some tension relief. Additionally, the movements and the energy they create, especially through the feet and legs, will aid in getting your mind and body to the zone.

An important point regarding movement is that you must be continuously building and maintaining energy through your feet and legs and up through your trunk. This energy generated then needs to transfer into your backswing. Therefore, your backswing is a seamless continuation of your last feet, leg and/or waggle movements, and as such, there is no break in energy. The greats had some movement just prior to, or at the start of their backswings to facilitate the transfer of energy, most typically in their legs or feet, whether it was the slightest push of a knee or foot movement.

VISUALIZATION & PHYSICAL FEEL STRENGTHENS FOCUS & CONCENTRATION

"You swing your best when you have the fewest things to think about."
                                                            -Bobby Jones-

The Swing (Phase Three)

As discussed, you need to understand that time and movement are two of the most critical elements of the Swing Phase. *The other two key elements, visualization and physical feel, are of the utmost importance, but since you should have rehearsed and established them in the Pre-Swing Phase, you are simply bringing them with you to the Swing Phase.* Further, with a strong visualization and physical feel being your sole thoughts in this phase, your focus will narrow and help you stay in the present.

As Bob Rotella asserts in his book, *Golf Is Not A Game Of Perfect*, "On the first tee, a golfer must expect only two things of himself: to have fun, and to focus his mind properly on every shot." He also added that, "Before playing any shot, a golfer must lock her eyes and mind into the smallest possible target," possibly meaning that a tight and narrowed focus is key to avoiding distractions. With our Swing phase, you should be able to achieve such a focus and concentration when you utilize the power of visualization and physical feel for the shot, within the specific 8-second time frame.

A narrowed focus is also a byproduct of the confidence and commitment once you begin to achieve the fundamentals from the first two phases. This was not only the essence of Hogan, but appears to be the case for a majority of the greatest players, both past and present. They were so fundamentally locked in, in part by their confidence, that they neither had the time nor the need to worry about anything else as they moved into their Swing Phase. They simply stepped up and hit the shot.

"I'm the best and I'll thank you to remember that."

-Harry Vardon-

When discussing the mental flow that occurs in the Swing Phase, it is important to note that it should be a short series of fleeting conscious thoughts and more subconscious actions. Again, in the Pre-Swing Phase, you've already established visualization, the "movie" for your shot (you see your start line, then the ball curving to your target) which you merged with your mental feel to obtain the physical feel (including mechanical swing thought(s)) through your "dress rehearsal" (practice swing(s)). Thus, there's relatively little conscious thought occurring during the Swing Phase. What small conscious thought(s) there might be should be playing the visualization, "movie," of the shot in your mind and sensing the physical feel (which includes mechanical swing though(s)) such as the soft or fleeting reminder to "maintain your spine angle" for example.

Once proficient and instinctive with the shot process, the only conscious thoughts you'll carry into the swing phase will be your shot visualization and physical feel. Your movements and timing will be instinctive (with little to no variation), thus no conscious thoughts (which will take some time to master) required regarding those two elements. *Understand that of the four key elements in the **Swing** phase, the only elements unique to any stock swing(s) is your visualization and physical feel.*

HOW TO PERFORM THE SWING PHASE

"… You need to step up and trust it …"
-Tiger Woods-

At the conclusion of Chapter 4, we end the Pre-Swing phase with you moving your lead foot into place to establish your stance while bringing with you a strong visualization and physical feel that you've established for the swing to be executed. By solely thinking of only these two elements, you should have tuned out all outside distractions. Now it's go-time.

The Swing Phase starts when your right foot is actively and initially placed, assuming you're a right-handed player (simply do the opposite if you're left handed). (Your feet should naturally fall where they feel most comfortable which will occur once you've learned a fundamentally sound address and stance so that it's instinctive.) Simultaneously, you should also place the clubhead behind the ball. Square the club face to the start line. Continuing on with your movement, you put your left foot where it naturally falls in your stance. From that position, check your feet and club face alignment by rotating your head to look down the start line and then to the target area to reaffirm your visualization. Simultaneously, perform a slight waggle of the club and adjust your right foot into its final place. Rotate your head back to the ball; then waggle the club to reaffirm your physical feel, simultaneously, shift your weight from foot to foot, and leg to leg to generate energy and help keep tension at bay.

Now, rotate your head a second time down the start line to the target to see a fleeting visualization and then rotate it back to the ball. Simultaneously, waggle the club a second time to affirm your physical feel and to relieve tension, simultaneously move your weight from foot to foot and leg to leg for energy. Once you complete the second waggle and weight shift, the club face comes back to the ball and the backswing starts within 1 to 1.5 seconds. With one last thought for your physical feel, the backswing starts and you swing through to the finish. The entire routine should take 8 seconds or less to complete.

You need to establish your own cadence in this phase regarding weight shifting, the number of waggles you prefer, how many times and when you rotate your head to picture the fleeting visualization. We recommend a weight shift from foot to foot and from leg to leg in conjunction with the waggle. It is important that you stay consistent from swing to swing. Repetitiveness is imperative. Again, take a look at the Swing Phases of Bobby Jones, Hogan, Tom Watson and Mickelson to see what we mean. (Golfs8SecondSecret.com)

If in this phase, you are not comfortable here with your stance, alignment, visualization, or feel, back off and restart from the Pre-Swing Phase, unless something needs to be re-considered from Information-Gathering, which dictates that you re-start from there.

Let's go into a bit more detail on the key physical movements of this phase.

The Waggle

Why waggle? Not only does it keep your physical feel engaged and provides one last opportunity to marry visualization and physical feel, but it also assists in releasing some tension and provides some energy.

In Ben Hogan's book, *Five Lessons – The Modern Fundamentals of Golf*, Hogan called the waggle, "The bridge between the address and the actual start of the backswing." He went on to explain its importance saying, "During the waggle, as he previews his shot and attempts to telegraph the mental picture from his brain to his muscles, the golfer makes the little adjustments necessary to be perfectly in balance. As he waggles, he tunes himself up and tones himself up for the swing."

Tom Watson, who like Hogan typically waggled twice on stock shots, said this in an article for *Golf Digest*:

"I see too many amateurs start the backswing from a static position. I think having a waggle before you start is important to avoid tension and establish good rhythm. Starting from a static position can *cause your grip pressure to change in stressful situations, and that makes it hard to swing the club freely."*

The waggle is done primarily with the wrists and forearms. The hands should remain reasonably centered over the ball, and the arms and shoulders should remain relaxed with only slight movement. You want to ensure that you have a comfortable pressure and feel on the grip.

Note: When performing the waggle, be careful not to change your spine angle. This can happen if you perform the waggle incorrectly.

Weight Shifting

While the waggle primarily affirms the physical feel and keeps your hands, wrists, and arms in motion, you must also keep your lower body engaged. *Keeping your feet, legs, and your hips engaged and energized is critically important (as discussed in the Movement section earlier) because they are a large source of power in the swing and help to relieve tension throughout the body.* The energy generated needs to be transferred to the backswing for a powerful swing. My recommendation is to be shifting your weight laterally from foot to foot, and leg to leg, with movement possibly carrying up to the hips. The weight shifting is of the utmost importance for it creates a stronger, freer, and more instinctive swing, especially under pressure.

Rotating Your Head

An issue that we need to address and is often overlooked by golfers is that they tend to lift their head when looking toward the target. This is incorrect for two reasons. First and foremost, by *rotating* your head instead of lifting it, your eyes and line of sight will travel over your ball and down your start line and through to your target uninterrupted. When lifting your head, your eyes and start line will not be properly aligned. A proper head rotation is essential to positively reinforce the accuracy of the visualization for your shot.

Secondly, lifting your head can change your posture and thus, your spine angle. Your body should be in the proper position already, so it makes no sense to change your posture by looking up at the target. Instead, you need to make sure you are not lifting your head at all, just rotating it as if it were on an axis. If you were looking from behind at a golfer doing the proper rotation, you would see that the level of the head does not move up and down from a rotation, thus maintaining the same posture throughout.

Question:

One Or Two Waggles, Looks, Sets of Weight Shifting?

The majority of the greats performed two waggles, two looks and two sets of weight shifting. However, several of them did one to one and a half waggles, one look and one set of weight shifting. It's a personal choice, but we recommend two waggles, two looks and two sets of weight shifting.

THE UNION

The end results from the Information-Gathering phase are: shot determination, initial visualization, mental feel, confidence, and commitment. Being committed to your club choice, target area, and strategy for the shot, you have built a strong mental feel and some initial physical feel. From there, you moved into the Pre-Swing phase where you further strengthened your feel when the visualization and mental feel is merged to obtain your physical feel (including mechanical swing thought(s)) through the practice swing(s). At this point, you should be even more confident and committed in your decision and your body should now be conditioned to execute the swing. In the Pre-Swing, the 12-second time limitation helped to encourage your mind to further eliminate distractions and narrow your focus into a more subconscious state, while the movements began to energize your body for athletic performance. The Swing phase is the union of the four key elements: visualization, physical feel, time and movement. You bring the visualization and physical feel from the Pre-Swing phase and a union is formed when encased and energized by the time limitation and movements. The result is more energy, less distraction, and a narrowed focus, leading to stronger, freer, more consistent, instinctive and reactive swings.

> *"A strong mind is one of the key components that separates the great from the good."*
>
> -Gary Player-

SUMMARY POINTS

- The four elements in the Swing phase are: the amount of time spent, continuous and rhythmic movement, visualization, and maintaining and strengthening physical feel. The most critical elements in this phase are time and movement.
- The Swing phase begins once your lead foot is initially placed to establish your stance. It ends upon completion of the follow through.
- The Swing phase should take strictly 8 seconds or less.

- The primary movements are the waggle(s) and weight shifting from foot to foot and leg to leg, and must be consistent, continuous and rhythmical
- The waggle acts as a bridge between the mind and body and provides the physical feel for the swing
- The weight shift between the feet, legs and possibly into the hips primarily provides energy and relieves tension in the swing.
- The energy created by your movements needs to be transferred to the backswing for a smooth and strong swing.
- Your mind should be focused solely on the shot visualization and physical feel which you carried over from the Pre-Swing phase. This helps narrow one's focus and stay in the present.

See video for this chapter at:
http://golfs8secondsecret.com/book-chapter-videos/

6

Concluding Remarks

One of the most historic shots in golf history was Ben Hogan's 2-iron (or 1-iron depending on whom you want to believe) approach shot at Merion on the 72nd hole of the 1950 U.S. Open. After struggling on the greens for much of the fourth round, and coming off of his third back-nine bogey at the 17th hole, Hogan came to the 458-yard par-4 18th needing to make a par to join a playoff with Lloyd Mangrum and George Fazio. After a perfect tee shot that finished in the middle of the fairway, he was left with a little more than 200 yards to the pin (given today's equipment technology, this equates to a 230 to 250 yard shot). Hogan stared down at the green and gathered the information that he needed to play the shot. When all the variables were weighed, he chose his 2-iron, and after his fluid and time efficient Pre-Swing Phase, he stepped into address. Within eight seconds he produced that classic Hogan swing and sent the ball soaring through the Pennsylvania air as a huge gallery watched anxiously. The ball came to rest 40 feet from the hole, and he two-putted to finish off a 74 that gave him a 72-hole score of 7-over-par 287 on a famously difficult course that had lived up to its billing all week.

Hogan outplayed Mangrum and Fazio the next day with a hard-fought 69 (in an 18 hole playoff) to earn his fourth major championship victory and second U.S. Open Championship trophy, yet not a single shot can be remembered from those 18 playoff holes more so than his 2-iron the day before, considered by many to be an absolutely perfect shot. In his book, *Five Lessons- The Modern Fundamentals of Golf,* Hogan wrote about that shot and revealed that his take on it was "markedly different" than that of the adoring public who defined him based on that one single swing.

"They are inclined to glamorize the actual shot since it was hit in a pressureful situation. They tend to think of it as something unique in itself, something almost inspired, you might say, since the shot was just what the occasion called for. I don't see it that way at all. I didn't hit that shot then – that late afternoon at Merion. I'd been practicing that shot since I was twelve years old. After all, the point of tournament golf is to get command of a swing which, the more pressure you put on it, the better it works."

Hogan indeed had control over his swing regardless of how intense the pressure was. This type of confidence and control over one's game is what golfers at any level are looking to achieve, the ability to play their best golf under any circumstance. Striving towards this Hogan-esque confidence will help any golfer achieve the ability to play their best golf.

Concluding Remarks

WHAT LED TO GOLF'S 8 SECOND SECRET

Over the years, I have observed and taught hundreds, possibly even thousands of skilled players. Some of them were very good, and others, exceptional. The best of them had excellent swing mechanics, but being as I have a very good understanding of sound swing mechanics, I know that excellent swing mechanics don't necessarily produce winners and champions. Obviously, there's only a very small group of players to ever reach the elite level. Our observations and research of the greats led us to the development of our shot process which we believe is a critical component in how and why Ben Hogan and the others were able to separate themselves from their fellow competitors.

ESSENTIAL QUALITIES

The greatest players possessed many special attributes. An offshoot from our observations, research and the development of our shot process is a list of essential qualities. What follows seem to be the characteristics of winners. Whether a golfer is seeking to win a club or state championship, a PGA Tour event, or even a Major Championship, we believe that these essential qualities are the shared characteristics of championship golfers.

- **Competitive Drive:** Not all golfers play the game at a highly competitive level, nor do all golfers have the desire to do so. Some play simply to enjoy the pleasures of the game. However, if a golfer seeks to play to the best of their ability, there seems to be a correlation between competition and better golf. For example, because some might have a never ending goal to win, they are more inclined to try to consistently elevate their game. While the process that we're teaching here can't ignite the competitive "fire" within you, it *can* help you to capitalize on good starts in both recreational and competitive rounds since it's designed to help you swing freely, and is the clearest and easiest way to do so under pressure and get near or to the zone.

- **Drive to Constantly Improve:** as alluded to before, this quality is connected to a golfer's competitive drive. If your goal is to win tournaments, then you will push yourself diligently to learn, practice and experience in order to achieve that goal.

- **Creativity on the Course:** The greatest golfers know how to maneuver the course in creative ways. They each have unique styles of navigating different situations and you should too, to best match your playing style. Creativity is largely formulated in the Information-Gathering phase, through mental feel, and executed through physical feel. After a round is over, you should get into the habit of reflecting upon your shots, taking special note of your unique shots and where you could have executed better and need to improve. This will help you to build and expand your knowledge and remember the experience.

- **Intense & Pointed Focus:** This trait is imperative to great golf. If your mind is wandering or focused on too many things, then you're much less likely to achieve the best results possible. Having a pointed focus helps one stay in the present. If you're focusing on future outcomes rather than current actions, then your focus is misplaced. As you should know by now, our shot process places a strong emphasis on being focused, especially during the Pre-Swing and Swing phases. By focusing on the strong command you obtained through visualization and producing a strong physical feel, you're able to limit distractions and produce freer, more instinctive and reactive swings. The time constraints in the Pre-Swing and Swing phases are key in confining and narrowing your focus.

- **Confidence:** This is the Holy Grail of golf. Trusting your talents and abilities has a number of benefits on the course, as we've discussed in the previous chapters. We have all heard this an innumerable amount of times. Our shot process helps to train you to be more confident from start to finish. Furthermore, you should find that this helps you to be less judgmental when the outcome isn't as desired.

- **Commitment:** This is the culmination of confidence. By being confident in your decisions in the Information-Gathering Phase and beyond, you are more inclined to *trust* your abilities which increases your commitment. By being committed to your shots, your less apt to question yourself which ties back into decreasing distractions and maintaining strong focus. In addition, you should be 100% committed to your shots but only use 80% effort in hitting them. Most golfers typically do the opposite. They're 80% committed and use 100% effort in hitting the shot. The elements of the Swing Phase help eliminate "trying too hard" which assists golfers by helping them to simply react instinctively.

- **Short Term Memory:** The greatest champions rarely let poor shots affect their mental fortitude. They viewed bad shots as an anomaly and not a pattern or a trend, otherwise that self-doubt would carry into ensuing shots and negatively affect their confidence. That's one of the reasons they rarely hit two bad shots in a row. Amateurs, on the other hand, tend to play teeter totter golf. That is, they try to make technical corrections after every poor shot. This leads to constantly stressing over one's mechanical swing thoughts and robs you of energy, visualization and feel. Over time, after implementing our shot process and working hard to improve your game, your confidence will grow, and as a by-product, you will experience less self-judgment on the course.

- **Rhythm:** Tempo and rhythm help create consistency and harmony, which in turn create a sense of security and habit on the course, and once again contribute to confidence. Our shot process emphasizes how critical it is to develop consistent time limitations, movements and a rhythmical cadence in the Pre-Swing phase and the Swing phase.

- **Sound Mechanics:** Though teaching the physical mechanics of a golf swing are beyond the scope of this book, it goes without saying that great golfers have sound mechanics. As such, we too maintain that you need to perform critical mechanical swing actions in certain ways.

- **Short Game Skills:** Similar to swing mechanics, this book does not directly address the short game. However, you *can* implement our shot process to aid your short game in and around the greens by establishing a routine for visualization, feel, and instinctive action.

- **Patience:** Results don't always come quickly or easily in the game of golf. Championship golfers dedicate their lives to the game and are constantly working to improve their game. They recognize that improvement takes time. Were they to get discouraged when the results didn't come fast enough, then we're sure they wouldn't have won the championships that they did. It takes time for the brain to develop new habits and rewire itself. A study published in the *European Journal of Social Psychology* found that it takes more than 2 months or around 66 days (of daily repetition) for something simple to become habitual. However, you should notice immediate improvement in the quality of your shots even though the entire shot process will take longer to become instinctive.

CONSCIOUSNESS

You may have noticed that many of the essential qualities that we've identified are related to the mental side of golf. Excellent mechanics have utmost value. That aspect of golf can't be disputed, but the mental side of golf is arguably the most important (after a certain level of skill is obtained).

We know of few champions that didn't have a top-notch mental game, but we can show you countless golfers with near perfect mechanics that cannot play championship level golf. It's the marriage between very good swing mechanics and a strong mental game that creates the greatest golfers.

One of the key mental components that will help to create a freer and more instinctive swing is the natural progression from conscious thought to a more subconscious, instinctive and reactive thought and feel. To help explain this better, let's consider a typical play in football.

First, the players are all huddled together where a specific play is being communicated to the other players by the quarterback. In each player's mind, they must consciously remember what the play entails, from blocking schemes to receiver routes. As they approach the line, they can mentally picture (visualization) their individual assignments. Once the ball is snapped however, their minds shift from a largely conscious state, where they were consciously thinking about the play, to more subconscious, instinctive and reactive actions as the play unfolds, where their bodies perform as they have been planning and practicing all along, and experience is critical.

If you compare this to our shot process, you can see a striking resemblance. In the Information-Gathering phase, you are largely conscious, thinking deliberately about the variables that could affect your shot while you are mentally creating a plan of action, or a play as in football. Then you progress into the Pre-Swing phase. Here you are rehearsing the shot and turning your conscious thoughts into a more subconscious feeling. Your trigger could be likened to the snapping of the ball, where everything begins to become more instinctive. Once in the Swing phase, your body performs with little conscious thought, except for the fleeting conscious recognition of your visualization and physical feel (mechanical swing thought(s)), just like a football player naturally running his route while thinking of the pattern.

THE ZONE

Earlier in this book we mentioned how Golf's 8 Second Secret shot process will give you the best chance and easiest pathway to get to the zone. The zone, as we described it, is a mental and physical state in which your mind and body instinctively work together at their highest capacity, which can produce your best performance. It is not a state that is easy to get into, nor will you experience it with great frequency, but our shot process will set you up to get into or near the zone more often, especially in those pressure filled situations when you need it most.

When you are playing competitive golf, you will naturally experience some degree of pressure which will typically increase if you are playing well in a competitive round or tournament. Pressure is a double-edged sword in that it can either wreak havoc on your game if improperly dealt with, or it can be the platform upon which your best golf is played. If you are confident in your game and you have a good start and pressure builds, then your body will begin to release adrenaline. This flow of adrenaline coupled with confidence and freer swings will help propel your mind and body into a state where your swing is more instinctive and reactive, and more times than not, everything fires properly.

When the expectancy to play well is affirmed by hitting the shots you want, then an even greater feeling of confidence will carry you over to perform the next shot in the same manner or even better (momentum). Before you know it, you will be executing excellent shots in a fluid and repetitive manner.

When playing well, and in or near the zone, you will tend to get excited and amped up. As long as you are aware of this and don't allow it to overwhelm you, this extra energy will not be detrimental (especially once you've experienced it a few times). After all, the stimulation from playing well is what helps you get to the zone in the first place. This strong level of intensity is different for every player. This is rarely discussed in detail by accomplished players and teachers, making it quite difficult to learn, further adding to the complexity of golfing in the zone. The more times you find yourself close to or in the zone, the more wisdom and experience you will take from those rounds which will make it easier for you to capitalize on similar opportunities down the road.

Overall, golfing in the zone is a wholly inclusive harmonization of every element of golf. Our shot process will help you in obtaining and maintaining this elusive and powerful psychological and physical state, as most of the greats must have achieved numerous times.

PRACTICE

"You can't go into a shop and buy a good game of golf."

-Sam Snead-

The good news is – and this is true no matter how you have executed and performed in the past, and especially under pressure – you can change and we're confident you will improve by adopting and practicing Golf's 8 Second shot process. Incorporating our shot process right away is recommended even though it will take some time for it to become second nature.

First, one should prepare to begin practice. To do this, you'll need to evaluate how well you execute the phases and elements within. We suggest that on paper you evaluate how you normally approach and progress through your typical shot process on the course. Do you already follow the three phases and the elements within? If not, why not? Ask yourself, "Does my physical routine and mental thoughts match up and give me the results discussed in this book? Do I tend to have some of the problems and issues that have been described i.e. lacking confidence and commitment, too many mental distractions, low emphasis on feel, too static, not properly energized, restricted swing, etc.?" Think through your shot process and take note of where you believe you are coming up short.

After you have made a thorough "paper examination" of your shot process, go to the practice range and have a friend or PGA Pro videotape (any smartphone should do the job) your entire shot process. Then specifically, the phases and elements within. Key issues to ask yourself, "Do I have a defined starting and end point for each phase? What's my timing? What movements do I make? Do I have a proper waggle(s)? Do I generate enough feet and leg movements to create sufficient energy to relieve tension? Do I visualize my shots? How strong is my physical feel?" Review both the paper analysis and video footage to identify your weaknesses and where you need the most improvement.

HOW TO PRACTICE THE SHOT PROCESS

Begin with the Swing phase

First, practice with a club in your hand, standing approximately 2 to 4 paces behind the ball. Walk to the ball and actively place your right foot in before setting the club head behind the ball. Once the right foot hits the ground the clock starts and the remaining address movements along with the entire swing need to take place in under 8 seconds or less.

We recommend you do at least 10 to 15 walkthroughs a day, whether it be at home, work, on the range, or a combination of them. Over time, the movements will start to become habitual. It is a good idea to try and aim, initially, for a 7 second time limit, especially if you have been slow in this phase because under pressure your natural tendency will be to take longer. We believe that good evidence of this was when Lee Trevino went to Killeen Municipal Golf Course in preparation for the 1972 British Open to be played at Muirfield. Trevino played his practice rounds at Killeen by hitting a shot, then sprinting to the next shot to be hit; the caddie was in a golf cart to keep up. Once Trevino arrived at his ball, he spent little to no time in the information gathering, pre-swing and swing phases, which would imply that he determined and hit his shots on feel and instinct. In those practice sessions, he simply ran up to the cart, grabbed a club, and swung. We're confident this helped him strengthen his mental feel for distance and other variables, and helped his swing become freer and more instinctive. He went on to win his second British Open later that month, beating Jack Nicklaus.

Once time and movement are more habitual than not, then add the visualization and physical feel. You'll know when you have learned the elements when they are instinctive instead of conscious, in walkthroughs and when actually hitting shots. Once that is achieved, move on to the Pre-Swing phase.

Practicing the Pre-Swing

As stated, the critical elements of the Pre-Swing phase are visualization and physical feel. To practice, go through the same routine you did to learn the swing phase. We recommend you do at least 10 to 15 walk throughs a day (all the way through to the swing phase). Standing 2 to 4 paces behind the ball, the Pre-Swing starts when you initiate your trigger, followed by a visualization and a practice swing or two to merge your visualization and physical feel. This is followed up with a brief visualization as you move uninterruptedly to establish your stance and start the Swing Phase. Check your 12 second time limit and get movements down so they're repetitive. Note, it's best to be quicker than 12 seconds versus slower than 12 seconds.

Again, you should see immediate results when hitting individual shots.

A reasonable goal would be to achieve the time limits and movements of the Pre-Swing and Swing phase so that they're substantially habitual without conscious thought within 60 to 90 days. As the great teacher Davis Love Jr. stated, *"A routine is not a routine if you have to think about it."* It will take longer to achieve proficiency under pressure, however, you should see a steady improvement in your results as your shot process becomes instinctive.

Concluding Remarks

PRACTICING VISUALIZATION & FEEL

Visualization

We believe that Visualization is the easiest element to learn and become proficient at. Our brains work best when there is something to see. For example, if we say orange to you, your brain will typically see a picture of an orange, the fruit, or it may see the color. Likewise in practice, if you say to yourself, my ball's start line is the right edge of the green and then draws left to the pin, your mind will see the ball flying through the air in that way. Verbalizing turns words into pictures, which helps you "see" the shot. If you go with either visualization as discussed in Chapters 3 & 4, you need to practice seeing the "movie" of your ball flying down your start line and then curving toward and ending at your target.

The best way to practice visualization is by replaying familiar holes and shots in your mind so that you can accurately visualize. Play at least 10 to 15 or more shots in your mind daily. Just before falling asleep is a good time to do this. Simultaneously, note how the images give your muscles a feeling for the shot. It has been documented that before tournaments, many great players will seclude themselves in a quiet place and visualize playing each hole of the course while taking note of the feeling that comes about. This is an extremely powerful tool and will help you obtain confidence, feel and focus.

Feel

Feel comes from playing golf itself, for it's learned primarily from practice, playing and experience. It is developed and strengthened by putting in your time. The more time you put in, the broader, more profound and instinctive one's feel will become. We recommend the following exercises to strengthen your mental and physical feel. When you go to the range, pick out various targets one at a time and estimate the distance. Using your range finder, see how close your estimate is to the actual distance. Mike Bender does this exercise with Zach Johnson, where they have a contest to see who can estimate the distance the most accurately. Next, hit some shots to those targets to practice converting your mental feel to a physical feel. If your skill level is such, hit high shots, low shots, fades and draws to those targets making sure to note the distance change with each type of shot (very important). Continue practicing this on a regular basis and you'll be impressed with how quickly and accurately you will be able to determine distance by sight only. This enhanced feel and instinctive skill will strengthen your confidence and improve your overall play.

In addition to having a feel for distance, one needs a strong feel for the effects of wind. One of the ways to practice this is on the range on windy days. Note the strength of the wind and then hit several shots with different clubs making sure to watch how they are reacting and the distance they are going. Depending on the size of your range tee, try to get in different locations in order to experience different wind directions and their effects on your shots. A practice range is typically a large area, so make sure to have precise targets and distances so that you can accurately see the effects the wind has on your shots. Pay close attention to the results as this will help you build a library of knowledge you can draw from when needed. As you become better at practicing in the wind and understanding its effects on the ball (from a conscious perspective), it will become more subconscious and instinctive on the course when you play, especially under pressure. Make this a priority in your range practice so that you can become better at calculating the wind, thus making better choices with your club selection and targets. Playing gives you the best opportunity to recognize whether or not you have a good understanding on the effects of wind on your shots. Make sure to keep track of patterns and distances of your shots in different wind directions and speeds. From our observations, players usually underestimate the loss of distance when hitting into the wind and come up short more times than not. In cross winds they underestimate the amount the ball will curve in the direction of the wind, thus missing their intended targets by a large margin. If you see these tendencies, make adjustments accordingly and add them to your library of knowledge for future use. Once your feel becomes stronger, the benefits will show through.

The greats succeeded in handling the variables time and time again when they needed to the most. Their feel was a key element for their shot success and championships.

Note: Research shows that shorter intervals of practice over longer periods of time are more effective than trying to "cram" this knowledge into a few grueling practice sessions. 10 to 15 minutes twice a day is probably better than 45 minutes once a day. Depending on the time you devote and your level of practice, you should see positive results right away, initially, in the quality of individual shots.

Tiger Woods at the 16th

One of the iconic shots that demonstrates visualization and feel is when Tiger holed his chip shot for birdie on the Par 3 16th hole in 2005 at the Masters on his way to winning his 4th Green Jacket. The skill to make that shot was born of dedicated practice, experience, and feel, but the execution was primarily instinctive.

PRACTICING INFORMATION GATHERING

"Success in golf depends less on strength of body than upon strength of mind."

-Arnold Palmer-

We believe part of Palmer's meaning of this is that a player needs to play smart (includes being experienced), be confident and committed to every shot to be played. What we find is that many competitive players don't fully understand the importance of this and we believe a thorough knowledge of the information gathering phase goes a long way towards achieving confidence and commitment. We know that many of the greats possessed far more knowledge than laid out in this book, for we could write another 10 or more pages on the nuances and situational knowledge for the Information Gathering phase alone. The information is out there, but you will need to spend time to search it out, and most importantly, learn it, practice it and then experience it.

If your goal is to play your best, we're sure you can appreciate that if you're in a 72 hole event and you end up winning in a playoff with a score of 270 or 290, a 1% advantage over 4 days is a big deal.

Thorough knowledge, practice, and experience will give you a winning edge.

GOLF'S 8 SECOND SECRET
INVERTED TRIANGLE DIAGRAM

(See Addendum A)

The purpose of this diagram is multi-fold. It illustrates how the mind moves from conscious thoughts to primarily subconscious thoughts and actions. It shows how the time limitation will decrease from phase to phase. The movements in the Pre-Swing tend to be more broad and loose as compared to the movements in the Swing phase which are more concise and deliberate. Visualization will be broader during Information Gathering and become tighter as you progress into the Swing phase. The progression of feel works its way from a mental feel into a strong physical feel.

GOLF'S 8 SECOND SECRET SHOT PROCESS FLOW CHART

(See Addendum B)

This flow chart shows the breakdown of the three phases and elements within the shot process, along with the benefits they yield.

THE FULL PICTURE

Golf's 8 Second Secret shot process that we have outlined has been tweaked through trial and error by the greatest players themselves. In particular, the process seems to have naturally and instinctively evolved from within the greats themselves. To us, it isn't coincidence that the process by which the greatest players played, could all mirror each other so closely, especially in the Swing Phase where little deviation exists among them regarding time limitations and athletic movement.

For decades the totality of the shot process has been under studied and under taught in golf. The goal of this book is to pass on this knowledge in a framework with details of Golf's 8 Second Secret shot process so that you can incorporate them and expand upon it as learned, practiced and experienced, with the goal of becoming the best player you can be. The men and women who've played our game at the very highest level likely know or knew- whether consciously or not- the principles we've advocated here. It's not too late for you to learn and adopt their methods. And in this case, time is on your side.

"You can always become better."

-Tiger Woods-

SUMMARY POINTS

- Golf is a complex game and better players consistently exhibit many of the essential qualities listed in this chapter.
- The ultimate benefit a player can obtain from our shot process is to get near or to the zone as often as possible. Once there, a player can surely reach or exceed their potential more times than not, which will give you a substantial edge over fellow players.
- The more knowledge one learns through study, practice and experience, the more you may find yourself having a competitive advantage. As such, Golf's 8 Second Secret shot process is another tool and guide to help you along with this objective.

See video for this chapter at:
http://golfs8secondsecret.com/book-chapter-videos/

Concluding Remarks

Addendum A

Inverted Triangle Diagram

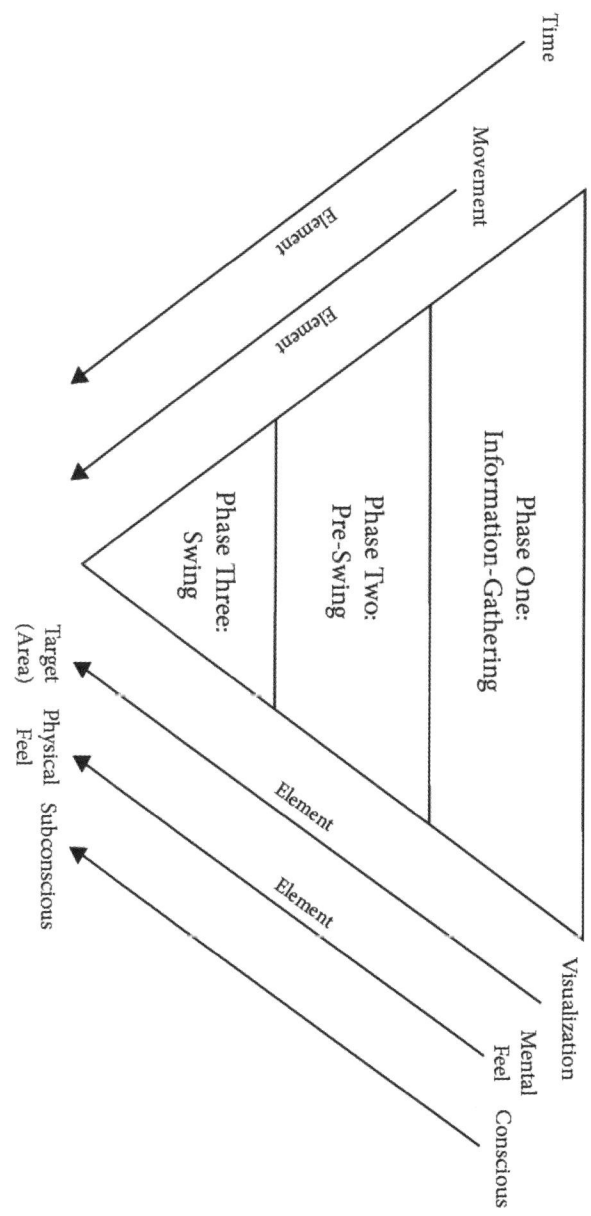

109

Addendum B

The Shot Process Flow Chart

1. Information Gathering Phase
a. Determine your target area, distance & analyze the variables (wind, elevation, lie, etc.)
b. Choose the type of shot, mental flight path (visualization) and club to be played
c. Start to acquire mental and physical feel for shot

 Building confidence & commitment for the shot

2. Pre-Swing Phase
a. Visualization of flight path to target
b. Merge visualization and mental feel (and mechanical swing thought(s)) with physical feel through a practice swing(s)
c. Athletic and sufficient movement to begin to energize and relieve tension
d. Time limit (12 seconds + or -)

 Shot's Execution

3. Swing Phase
a. Time limit (8 seconds)
b. Continuous & rhythmic movement, carried through to backswing
c. Visualization of flight path to target
d. Physical feel (and mechanical swing thought(s))

Yields

Confidence and commitment, athleticism/energy, decreased mental distractions, freer, more instinctive & reactive swings

 Results in less self-judgment after shots

Higher quality golf shots, more consistent play, and lower scores and the ability to play your best under pressure

 The Zone

ACKNOWLEDGMENTS

The publication of this book reflects the efforts of a team, and their effort and work is greatly appreciated. We would like to thank the following people for making this book become a reality: Mark Balen, for his vision and support when the initial concept was developed over a pint in a Scotish Pub; Sal Maiorana, for taking on the project in its infancy, and with only an outline, he developed the layout for the book; Alek Santiago, whose understanding of golf, writing, editing, and patience enabled us to finish this book; Connor Smith, whom we suspect has never seen and probably will never see a mountain he couldn't climb, the depth he provided to this book was significant; Jason Bender, for his skills in developing the website and the videos within; Bob Carney, for his thoughts and editing; Tom Kircher, for his input and editing skills; Andrea, for her editing and continuous support throughout this project; Jake Walsh, for the cover design; and last but not least, we would like to thank Llama for his enthusiasm for life, golf, and Lee Trevino, which provided significant insight for the book.